The Student's Music Library—Historical and Critical Studies

Edited by Percy M. Young, M.A., Mus. D.

THE LITERARY BACKGROUND TO BACH'S CANTATAS

Title page of the original edition of Cantata 71, written for a Council Election ceremony. Although a cantata, it is called 'Motet': other cantatas—particularly secular ones—bear such titles as *Dramma per musica*.

Glückwünschende Kirchen MOTETTO.

als
bey solennen Gottesdienste/ in der Haupt-Kirchen B. M. V.
der gesegnete Raths-Wechsel/
am 4. Februarii dieses M. D. C. C. VIII. Jahres geschah/

und die Regierung
der Käyserl. Freyen-Reichs-Stadt
MÜHLHAUSEN/
der Väterlichen Sorgfalt des Neuen-Rahts/
nemlich/

Des Hoch-Edlen/ Vesten/ Hochgelahrten
und Hochweisen Herrn/

Herrn Adolff
Streckers/

und
des Edlen/ Vesten/ und Hochweisen Herrn

Hn. Georg Adam
Steinbachs/
beyderseits Hochverdienten
Herrn Bürgermeistern/
wie auch
derer übrigen Hoch- und Wohl-ansehnlichen
Mitgliedern/
freudig überreichet wurde/
schuldigst erstattet/
durch
Johann Sebastian Bachen/
Organ. Div. Blasii.

Mühlhausen/
druckts Tobias David Brückner/ E. HochEdl. Rahts Buchdr.

THE LITERARY BACKGROUND TO BACH'S CANTATAS

James Day

LONDON: DENNIS DOBSON

Set in Great Britain by Santype Ltd, Salisbury
Printed in Great Britain by
Clarke, Doble & Brendon Ltd., Cattedown, Plymouth

To L. W. F.

Lucerna pedibus meis . . .

CONTENTS

ix

ILLUSTRATIONS

FOREWORD

There is very little in the nature of original discoveries in this book—if anything at all. What, I believe, is new is the attempt to correlate baroque elements in the texts of Bach's cantatas with baroque elements in the music. It has always seemed strange to me that so little has been done in this field, and it is patently absurd to use what has now become such an emotive term as *baroque* in the two arts of music and literature (to say nothing of its use in the plastic arts, *via* which the term first came to be used in literature) without trying to find out if there are any parallels between the two uses of the terms. This is all the more the case when we think how much of Bach's work consisted in the setting to music of programmatic texts.

My thanks are due to Dr Percy Young for suggesting that I undertake the work, to Professor Leonard Forster, whose zeal and scholarship have been at my disposal since I first became interested in baroque literature as an undergraduate, and who has made a number of valuable suggestions concerning secondary sources for it, and last, but not least, to my wife for her help in preparing the index and her encouragement and advice.   J.D.

Basel,
Switzerland,
February 26*th*, 1959

I. SOME IMPORTANT FEATURES OF GERMAN BAROQUE LITERATURE

From the time of the Reformation onwards, the pattern of social change within the Holy Roman Empire was for many years arbitrary rather than organic, and this had an important bearing on the status and function of the writer and the poet who lived and worked within its borders. The final result of the Peace of Augsburg was worse than the confused state that existed before it. The outstanding feature of that treaty had been the right granted to each Estate of the Realm, to each Prince and Free City, to choose between Catholicism and Protestantism, and to ensure that within its domains the chosen faith was observed. This had marked a further decline in the central authority of the Empire, for it admitted that religion, hitherto the concern of that Empire as a whole, now became yet another of those items delegated to the mercy of smaller powers. The result was that land-grabbing in the name of religion, a marked feature of pre-Augsburg politics, remained in effect unaltered, culminating in the Thirty Years' War, which disrupted the Empire as a coherent political unit for ever, and marked the first stage in the passing of pan-German hegemony from Catholic Austria to Protestant Prussia. The war itself was not responsible for the chaos of seventeenth-century political life; it merely aggravated certain tendencies which had been inherent in that life for many years, and it is one of the terrible ironies of history that the final outcome of Luther's attitude to politics was at least as responsible for the confused and atomistic nature of baroque political life as the theories of that Machiavelli whom Lutheran baroque moralist writers, such as Weise, Rist, and on occasion Gryphius and Schottel, condemned as wicked and subversive.

At the outset of the Reformation, the Lutheran Church had found itself in an unhappy predicament. It had to tie itself to an existing social order or perish. Calvinism, as an organized religious movement, laboured under no such disadvantage, and was free to create its own mercantile oligarchy. It is interesting that while Calvinist princes were influential and quite numerous in seventeenth-century Germany—the most notable of course being the Hohenzollerns—Calvinism as an organized movement, related to a particular class of society, was not. Nor was Lutheranism very successful outside Germany, save in Scandinavia.

All conditions therefore conspired to reduce the middle classes to a state of cultural dependence on the aristocracy, whose satellites they tended to become politically. They did not, as in Holland, become rich patrons of the arts; their economic position was far too precarious; a series of ruinous inflations from 1557 onwards, and external political events, such as the sack of Antwerp in 1585, the closing of the London Steelyard (1598) and the secession of the Spanish Netherlands from Spain hit North German and South German cities alike. Any writer who wrote for a middle-class audience aimed at pleasing scholars, administrators, or professional men rather than mercantile patrons. And he wrote, not in order to earn a living—for he was generally a scholar or an administrator himself—but for other reasons which vary from writer to writer. For all the fulsome dedications and poems written in honour of great princes (and we shall see that they have a particular bearing on the nature of some of Bach's secular libretti) it was the minor nobility, upon whom much administrative responsibility devolved, who were the patrons of such writers as Gryphius (1616–64) and Opitz (1597–1639) during their years of travel and study abroad, where such patronage was forthcoming at all, and in the cases of Opitz and Gryphius, that patronage was for services rendered as family tutors.

None the less, certain remnants of the middle-class tradition which in the sixteenth century had supported such artists as Dürer or Urs Graf, and produced such writers as Hans Sachs—plying two trades and probably excelling in neither—did persist in such towns as Nuremburg and Danzig, for example, but there is no single thread running through the entire literature of the seventeenth century such as gives it a symptomatic unity of style. There are, however, certain reflections of ideas and attitudes which material conditions made acceptable—indeed essential—to the *literati*, and which were treated in different ways by different writers. The best summary of these ideas and attitudes available in English is Professor Leonard Forster's inaugural lecture: *The Temper of German Seventeenth-Century Literature*, and the viewpoint of the present chapter derives largely and quite unashamedly from his.

The conception of the independent literary artist, responsible only to his aesthetic sense and creative urge, is a comparatively recent one. The German baroque writer was not in this position at all; had he been so, he would have died of starvation even earlier than the expiry of the short life-span which seems to have been allotted to many of his kind. Patronage was erratic; royalties non-existent. Payment for publications was ridiculously small, and in any case, few of the important writers produced enough to live by. He needed another post to live by while he wrote during his leisure. He might be a civil servant, such as Gryphius or Lohenstein (1635–83) became; he might be a pastor, like Gerhardt (1607–76) or Rist

(1607–67), a schoolmaster, like Weise (1642–1708), a land administrator, like Grimmelshausen (1622–76), or even a land-owner, like Anselm von Ziegler (1663–96), but in only one case—that of Philip von Zesen (1619–89)—is it assumed that the writer lived by his pen, and that on the purely negative ground that no other source of income open to him has been discovered up till now.

So all notions of baroque poetry being necessarily the outcome of personal emotional experience should be regarded with scepticism, and the merits of such poetry assessed from standards rather different from our own. It is true that Opitz recommended[1] that poetry should be the outcome of inspiration and experience—but his interpretation of the Greek word *enphantasiotos* implied the ability to display a ready wit, to coin far-fetched conceits, and to draw a topical moral from them. It was the custom to display a vast learning; annotations, prefaces, and references to other poems, and direct quotations from classical authors—particularly Seneca—abound. Criteria of judgment were those of erudition rather than originality, in which the writer was as a rule hardly interested. The aim of literature was twofold—*instruire* and *plaire*.

The seventeenth century saw the imposition of new formal patterns on vernacular literature. The artist-craftsman of the Hans Sachs type has already been

B

mentioned. The kind of verse he wrote persisted up till the last decades of the sixteenth century—and in some cases much later; Christian Reuter (1665–1715?), for example, produced a Passion oratorio in the old forms as late as 1708. But in general, metres and forms accepted by baroque writers were those suggested by Martin Opitz in his *Buch von der teutschen Poeterey*, of 1624. Opitz followed the model of the Pléiade. As Forster states[2], Opitz was more important as an example to other poets rather than for what he achieved himself, and it should be remembered that he was no Malherbe. His reforms did not aim at banishing exaggerations and vulgarisms, but at producing formal models for learned poets to imitate, and anyway, despite the numerous societies formed in Germany in the seventeenth century for the preservation and improvement of the German language, the lack of a central administration deprived German literary reformers of any impetus such as the Académie Française was to provide from Paris. Opitz really brought up to the surface of the German language the learned humanistic current which had been flowing underground, as it were, in the scholarly Latin lyric of the sixteenth century.

Nor was Opitz the only one to try this; Weckherlin (1584–1653) and Höck (1573–1618), for example, in their different ways, sought other solutions to the same problem. But in the main, it was Opitz's solution which prevailed. He was not a great, nor even an original writer, and he certainly laid no great stress on originality in the precepts he laid down. His example encouraged what we may call part-time poets working along highly academic lines, and that is what many baroque poets were.

If it can be said that Opitz took his lead from the French lyric, it can also be said that he encouraged the adoption of Latin models in other forms. This was particularly so in the case of drama, where he urged the adoption of Senecan models, with their compound of rhetoric, violence, and moralizing. His definition of tragedy in his handbook (referring the reader to Aristotle and Daniel Heinsius if he would know more) refers in particular to the part played by murders, patricides, arsons, wars, uproars, calamities, and so on. But in the preface to his translation of Seneca's *Women of Troy*, he points out[3] that a tragedy 'is nothing but a reflection of those who draw sustenance from pure chance in all their actions and ways'. (He adds, on the next page, that it helps to inculcate stoic constancy in those who watch or read it.) This viewpoint was taken over and modified by the two main writers of verse-tragedy in the century, Andreas Gryphius and Daniel Caspar von Lohenstein.

Seneca was a particularly suitable model for the age; his stoicism suited the serious-minded scholar with moral aims in his writing, particularly if he was a

Lutheran. Luther's dogma of justification by faith had secularized the world of time and space. What man *did* was irrelevant to his salvation; what mattered was what he *believed*. Moralists seeking to justify noble actions were compelled to find existential rather than religious grounds for their moral system. Small wonder that, in the seventeenth century, it was to the stoics that they turned in their endeavour to formulate a relevant, practical, and dignified form of conduct. The general uncertainty, the inscrutability of time, social chaos, and suspicion in personal relationships, led even scholars to interpret the world less in terms of cause and effect than in the realm of the occult and the irrational. Scepticism became an almost cynical evaluation of human motives and practices; life was explained in terms of the bizarre and the fantastic. History books published at the time often read like Old Moore's Almanac, chronicling the merely startling alongside the significant, and giving equal prominence to both.

Among the learned classes, the explanation of human affairs most generally accepted was that of the workings of Fortune. This is found even in correspondence between friends. The eminent grammarian, Büchner, wrote[4] to his friend Rudolph Brandt, for example, on October 14th, 1639, that it was as vain to protest against Fortune as against God— she was His instrument. Whether she is so regarded, or whether she is regarded as a *Dea destructiva* in her own right, it is her activities, as they impinge upon human life from moment to moment, that are examined and expounded in much baroque literature. In the seventeenth century, it is particularly the suddenness and the momentary impact of her frequently hostile and always capricious behaviour that attracts attention. In a number of cases, a serious attempt was made to compound the ethical teachings of stoicism, regarded as particularly relevant to the life of a learned administrator in an age dominated by uncertainty, with orthodox religious belief. Secular (stoicism) and sacred (Christianity), pagan (Seneca) and biblical elements were combined. Stoic constancy in the face of misfortune and mutability was sometimes regarded as an essential element in the retention of faith in God. Indeed, the practising of a stoic code of honour and conduct became regarded almost as an outward and visible sign of Christian beliefs. In Andreas Gryphius's tragedies, for example, particularly in *Catherina von Georgien* and *Carolus Stuardus*, we have striking examples of this.

Moreover, it was not difficult to find scriptural passages commending or pointing towards the stoic ideal; certain of the Psalms and most of the Book of Job could be cited in support of it. It is not therefore surprising that the same learned poets who avidly read Seneca and Justus Lipsius should find that their teachings were in no way inconsistent with the duties demanded of a Christian by the situations of his earthly life.

Sacred and secular, popular and learned elements met on other planes, too. Manfred Bukofzer, in his *Music in the Baroque Era*, points out how this happened in the case of one particular chorale, *O Haupt voll Blut und Wunden*.[5] The melody came from Hassler's love song *Mein G'müt ist mir verwirret*, published in 1601, and was fitted to the words of *Herzlich tut mich verlangen*. The Catholics used the same tune for the Latin hymn *Salve caput cruentatum*, which in turn was translated and paraphrased by Paul Gerhardt into *O Haupt voll Blut und Wunden*. There was no sharp division on the moral plane between pagan and Christian, and, as we shall see, elements from both secular and sacred literature found their way into the minor dramatic forms of the early eighteenth century, of which the Cantata was one.

The nature of baroque drama was complex and essentially unclassical. The forms and trappings derived in large measure from Seneca, by way of Opitz and the Dutch dramatists Hooft and Vondel. The stoic ethic, integrated to a greater or lesser extent with Christianity, derived from the same writer, again through the same Dutch poets, and also Justus Lipsius. The emphasizing of the action of Fortune and the element of chance in human life, and the remedies proposed in the face of the dangers they occasioned, varied from writer to writer. The Jesuits were content to point out the fact that Fortune's darling in this world might well be Satan's companion in the next. Gryphius tried to show that any attempt to exploit Fortune in this world was dangerous, because it would imperil the eternal fate of one's soul, by involving one in the pursuit of an illusion. Later on in the century, Lohenstein took over the violent external trappings, the peripeteia and rhetoric of Gryphius, divorced them from the stoic content which underlay them, and endeavoured to portray a world of seething political activity dominated only by the most accomplished actor or the most shrewd manipulator of other human beings. It is noteworthy, however, that all Lohenstein's dramas describe epochs and countries where the absence of any form of stoic or Christian conduct is to be expected, and that in a number of cases he points out that such conditions do not apply in modern Germany. In none of these cases can there be any attempt at organic development of character. The philosophical background of the plays implied that such a thing was impossible. In Gryphius, the central action revolves around the unshakable constancy of the idealized hero or heroine; in Lohenstein the tag that 'All the world's a stage' is true in a special sense—all the characters are putting on an act all the time, so that nobody can possibly know what the reality of a person, his essence and true nature, actually resembles.

The problem of *Sein und Schein*, reality and illusion, is not to be found only in the drama; it is a feature of nearly all baroque literature, verse and prose. The world is an illusion; either it deflects men's attentions from their eternal goal, or else its glories and achievements can be overthrown in a moment of time. The parodox of death leading to life, familiar to Christians in all ages, is particularly welcomed by an age which delighted in pointing out the illusory nature of all human affairs. The moral is nearly always implicit in the thematic material, even if it is not always explicitly stated. It is clothed in allegory, related in anecdote, expounded in argument. But the essence of the problem underlies almost all seventeenth-century German literature: in a world where so much is illusion, what can one accept as real?

A temper of mind which expects the unexpected comes in turn almost to welcome it, when a truth has become a truism. Thus although stoicism was a valid and perhaps essential system in the earlier part of the century, it often came to be just an accepted formula by the end of it. Writers' delight in paradox expressed itself now perhaps in formal tricks such as the long enumerative rhetorical structures, each superlative being overtrumped by a subsequent one, so beloved of baroque writers. So unreality at times seems to take on the air of being the only reality that some writers can accept, and they sometimes seem to accept it because it pleases them to do so. But in other cases, they aim at an 'unreality' of quite another order. This is the case in particular with the mystical writers of the age.

Enough has been said by way of introduction to indicate why mysticism should have made a particular appeal to people in Germany in the seventeenth century. Where all around him is mutable, where all authority is arbitrary, and where the individual feels isolated, then he will seek his own way to God because he will mistrust the rulings and dogma laid down by others. Just as the stoic conquers his passions and ambitions, remaining true to himself when all else fails him, and (if he is a Christianized stoic) steadfast in his faith so that he goes to Heaven, so the mystic looks within himself in a search for the God that others are not competent to reveal to him. Angelus Silesius (1624–77), Friedrich von Spee (1591–1635), Jakob Böhme (1575–1624), Quirinus Kuhlmann (1651–89), Johannes Arndt, Daniel Sudermann, Maximilian Scandaeus, Daniel von Czepko (1605–60), and Catharina Regina von Greiffenberg (1633–94) represent various kinds of mystical outlook, varying from a kind of rational whimsicality to a fervent ecstasy which borders at times on madness.

The slender connecting link which appears to bind these writers to the more orthodox Christians and the non-Christian stoics seems to be the curious conception that they nearly all had of Time. It is a commonplace of mystical tradition that the Eternal can be realized in an instant; Eternity is, in fact, a timeless instant to the mystic. In the seventeenth century, the significance of the instant, the *occasio*, is a key-theme in all branches of literature. Whether it is the motif of 'gather ye rosebuds while ye may', or of 'Watch, for ye know not when your Lord cometh', the sombre warning is never far absent. 'Use every instant, fill it with meaning; for no man knows how many more instants he will live.' The interplay of illusion and reality in a cosmos of unintegrated instants is not merely an excuse for spectacle, but often a problem, the solution of which answers to an intellectual or existential need.

From the two streams of mysticism and baroque stoic Christianity flowed a movement which gained much ground towards the end of the century, and which left its mark in certain of Bach's church cantata texts. Pietism emphasized the inner experience of Christ through the word of God, and enjoined the individual to be still and passive, to wait on His coming. This coming was not an apocalyptic matter, but essentially—like the constancy of the stoic, or the 'eternal moment' of the mystic—one concerning the individual's inner self. The two most important figures connected with pietism were Jakob Spener

(1635–1705) and August Hermann Francke (1663–1727). Spener asserted that Christians should follow an inner light, and that special groups of the Elect should be formed; this obviously threatened to contravene the religious settlement in the Peace of Westphalia of 1648, which divided the country between Lutherans and Catholics. The pietists claimed that scriptural exegesis, however learned, was as nothing. It had no effect on inner illumination. What mattered was prayer and edification. They thus had little use for learned sermons and theological hair-splitting; they tended to rely on individual emotional experience, almost invariably preceded by a spiritual night of gloom and despair. Whereas such a writer as Gryphius sees the human soul as a battleground between desires (which are illusions) and Christian stoic virtue (which is reality), the pietist sees it as one between light and darkness. Stoic constancy in facing misfortune becomes patient passive waiting on the call of God, *which always comes suddenly*, and often when it is least expected. According to Kurt Berger[6], the moment of conversion (and its suddenness and swiftness necessitate its being a moment; the vital and permanent metaphysical *Glückswechsel* determining the fate of a human soul) was almost invariably preceded by a sense of complete despair and uncertainty.

By 1695, pietism had penetrated to some twenty-five German cities, some twenty-five regions of the

Empire, and had more or less taken charge of the theological faculty of the University of Giessen, and Francke, demanding 'spontaneous' sermons, self-discipline, an abandonment of the world, individual recognition and interpretation of the word of God, and a puritanically spartan life, was engaging in theological disputations with the orthodox theologians of the University of Leipzig. Such a movement as Pietism would obviously decry elaborate baroque learning, and cultivate simple, emotive religious verse based upon the feelings of the converted rather than the misgivings of the moralist. Stoic individualism, the code of the proud pessimist, seeing the world as a vale of tears and putting on a bold face against it, since he cannot control its hostility, gives way to the more positive, optimistic individualism of the converted pietist singing ecstatic praise to the God on Whom he has not waited in vain. From suffering and death are drawn sweetness and light.

Yet although the baroque formulae lost much of their content, the baroque tricks and images retained their hold. Life as a stage, life as a journey, with the soul at the mercy of the winds (often controlled by Fortune); these two images in particular caught the fancy of baroque writers and the latter survived into the eighteenth century.

The theme of *navigatio vitae* was medieval in origin. It is well known to us from the Christmas hymn *I saw three ships*. There is a German version[7] : *Uns kommt ein Schiff gefahren*, attributed to the medieval mystic Johannes Tauler (c. 1300–71). In it, the cargo is the Virgin Mary, the mast the Holy Ghost, the sail is Love; in a contemporary Low German version, the cargo was Christ and the ropes were Love. The secular humanist counterpart was Fortuna's ship, or sometimes Venus's. Other variants existed, such as Sebastian Brant's *Ship of Fools* (1494), which was adapted and translated into English by Barclay in 1509. Caspar Barth, in the seventeenth century, wrote a poem about the Muses' Ship.

In the seventeenth century, the image was usually connected with the unpleasantness and uncertainty of a sea-voyage, with consequent dangers of storms and so on. In the allegory, these stood for passions or emotions. The ship is usually the individual soul, though Rumpius (in 1609), Josua Stegman (1627), and Simon Dach (1642) write of the ship of the Church. August Buchner (1628) refers to the waves of human desires; faith is the steersman. Variations of this treatment occur throughout the century; Gryphius, Rist, and David Peck (in *Wenn wir in höchsten Nöthen seyn*) being examples of poets who followed this fashion. In the realm of secular literature, the image was also common, though in this case, the destination of the voyage was of course not Heaven, as it was bound to be in the religious usage. In the love-lyric, for example, the lover is fancied as drifting helplessly on the sea of life when he has no beloved in whom to anchor his hopes; requited love is sometimes the port of destination. In at least one other case, the ship is sailing for Honour, and in one interesting case towards the end of the century, in a poem by Asmann von Abschatz (1646–99), the port is that of Fortune, meaning, in this case, the joys of requited love.

The detailed explanation and interpretation of an allegorical metaphor such as the above, a procedure dearly beloved by baroque writers, gives us some idea of the way in which metaphor and image were used in German baroque literature. A metaphor is usually a figure, an image, or a symbol which elucidates an idea by expressing it in easily imaginable concrete terms. But, as Dr. H. K. Kettler remarks[8] :

The baroque metaphor, however, pursues a different aim. It does not pretend to be a substitute for the original object or conception. Based neither on intuition nor on observation, the baroque metaphor, the product of a rationally calculating imagination, is either an abstraction of some minor quality of an object as the essence of the object itself, or an attempt to connect with each other the most contrasting phenomena. . . . Direct, harmonious relation between content and form ceases; colossal expenditure of form is needed for conveying the briefest content . . .

This does not necessarily imply that the metaphors used by baroque writers are inept or inappropriate; it does imply, however, that comparisons of the most far-fetched kind were pressed into service as images, and that exaggeration and lengthy enumerations are stylistic features of baroque form. This is particularly seen in the work of the so-called second Silesian school, including writers such as Hofmann von Hoffmanswaldau (1618–79) and Lohenstein. Silesia was the centre of two lively literary movements in the seventeenth century. The first began with Opitz, and reached its apogee in the work of Gryphius, who died in 1664. The second, drawing its inspiration from the elaborate and mannered style of Italian writers such as Marini, flourished at the end of the third and beginning of the fourth quarter of the century, though works of some of its writers were admired and imitated well into the eighteenth century. Indeed, Kettler mentions four works published between 1708 and 1718 which recommend Lohenstein's elephantine novel *Arminius* as an arsenal for plots and images. The more far-fetched the images sounded, the more fanciful and imaginative the writer was believed to be. Thus it is beside the point for a critic to observe that when one of Bach's librettists (Picander?) is using the metaphor of the world as a hospital, he is being quite coarse[9] ; quite apart from the fact that the image was not unknown in earlier poetry (Dach uses it, for example), Picander's image, and the enormous number of side-images he draws from it, would be regarded as *scharfsinning* and fanciful. The bombast and exaggeration were more than a tendency to useless ornament and to bad taste. They were an attempt to instruct and astonish the reader.

Ornament and indirect statement were however a recognized part of baroque style. Kettler[10] gives a quotation from a theoretical work by J. G. Neukirch (1724) indicating five different ways of saying 'He is false':

(1) Who harbours honey in his mouth and gall in his heart.

(2) Who speaks differently from his thoughts.

(3) Who coats his false words with sugar.

(4) His mouth gives forth honey, his heart poison and gall.

(5) He kisses us like Jacob, and stabs our heart with a dagger.

As Opitz had done before him, Neukirch was here setting an example which he intended to be followed. Oddly enough, baroque poetic theorists warned against over-elaboration in verse—even Hoffmanswaldau himself did so. And when Männling, in 1704, warned against 'dragging metaphors in by the hairs', he chose none other than Lohenstein, whom we should nowadays regard as the high priest of bombast, as the shining example of what to do.

It is therefore useless to expect any spontaneous,

natural romantic reaction to nature from baroque writers. The out-of-doors for them means the formal landscape garden—as a means to assimilating stoic constancy; a kind of philosophic sacrament of the open air—or the spa. When Opitz wrote an ode called *Zlatna*, he was careful to sub-title it 'Or—Tranquillity of the mind'. In it he describes, at considerable length, the virtuous Arcadian life and freedom from care of the idyllic Transylvanian spa town. In each case, the value of an object, an image, or an action, lies in its symbolic associations—not what it *is*, but what it *implies*, is the standard by which it is judged.

The bearing of all this on texts designed for music may well be imagined. First of all, it was the associative aspect of words that attracted some baroque composers—Bach among them—just as it was the associations of a word, and image, or an action, which were important considerations for baroque poets. Texts of the kind that such a mental attitude would engender would invariably offer opportunities for musical elaboration. This question will be considered in more detail later. Music was regarded—as we shall see—as an integral part of baroque dramatic spectacle. Lyrics, especially those such as were written by Simon Dach and his friends, were frequently intended to be performed to a musical setting, often one composed by the writer himself. It is reasonably likely that many of the 'Arien' which form such a conspicuous feature of such anthologies as Neukirch's (1697–1734; 7 volumes) were written with a musical setting in mind. A feature of the long, elaborate, and complex baroque tragedies was a solemn ballet-like chorus at the end of each act. In the case of the Dutch writers, these choruses were almost certainly set to music; it seems likely that in Gryphius's dramas the same held good.

The above chapter should in no way be regarded as a summary of all that was important in German baroque literature; it is merely an attempt to set out those aspects of that literature which are in some way relevant to the texts, both sacred and secular, which Bach was required to set. It would require far more than one chapter to expound the main features of the German literature of the seventeenth century, and it is fatally easy to label a certain characteristic as 'baroque' and to bind oneself as a slave to one's terminology. But if the word is to signify anything at all as a positive stylistic term, then we must be clear what temper of mind certain important writers of the seventeenth century possessed. It would be wrong to assert that all of them possessed all the qualities or assumed all the attitudes which I have tried to set out here, and it would be equally wrong to assume that I have given all the characteristics, or even all the important characteristics, of German baroque literature. Yet, as we shall see, they certainly occur in various guises in Bach's libretti, and there is evidence that he himself regarded some of them as more than mere tags and clichés.

II. THE CHURCH CANTATAS

According to Tagliavini[1], the first printed collections of sacred cantata texts appear to have been published in the 1670s; he particularly mentions Conrad Christian Dedekind's *Neue Geistliche Schauspiele*, published in 1670 and his *Heilge Arbeit über Freud und Leid* of 1676. Certain texts, too, in Michael Konghel's *Belustigung . . . aus allerhand Geist- und Weltlichen Gedicht-Arien*, published at Stettin in 1683, appear to foreshadow some of the cantata texts of the eighteenth century, and in 1698, Christian Gryphius, the son of the great Andreas Gryphius, published a collection of *Musikalische Andachten* which includes a number of verses 'written in the French manner in free verses'—quasi-recitatives, in fact.

Cantatas as a liturgical component in the church services were certainly known in Leipzig from the time of Sebastian Knüpfer (1657–76) onwards[2]. They were not, however, known under that name, and it was the custom, even in Bach's own day, to refer to the cantata as a 'Stück' or a 'Concerto'. The former word is used in German not only to mean a 'piece', but also, like the French 'pièce', when used with reference to a theatrical spectacle, a 'play'. As far as can be judged from a study of Bach's own texts, the cantata's function was liturgical and didactic; the majority of his cantatas are simple sermons set to music. The argument is delivered in the form of an exposition, or even in that of a small dramatic scena, and the point of departure is almost always the Gospel for the Sunday on which the cantata was performed. The music was clearly intended both to sugar the didactic pill and to be part of a liturgical action. It fulfilled this function by underlining and decorating important words in the text, as will be seen later, and the manner in which this was done is interesting. Quite often, Bach appears to have aimed at a dramatic effect—but not in the sense that Handel or Mozart employed music dramatically; his idea of drama, as we shall see, corresponded much more closely to that of the German baroque dramatists, being rhetorical and sententious, working on the plane of ideas rather than that of personalities.

Bach's church cantata texts fall quite naturally into five types. The first type consists of those composed entirely of verses taken from the Bible; an example of this type is No. 196 in the Bachgesellschaft edition, the Wedding Cantata, *Der Herr denket an uns*, which consists of four numbers—a chorus, a soprano aria, a duet for tenor and bass, and a final chorus. The text is extremely simple; it consists of verses 12 to 15 of Psalm 115, which centre around the idea of blessing. — It is natural enough that verse 12 should be set as a chorus, as the reference is to a collective— 'us', i.e. the House of Israel. The following soprano aria handles the idea of the Lord blessing both great and small; the duet calls down the blessing of the Lord upon 'ye and your children', and the final chorus assures the newly-wedded couple that they are the blessed of the Lord Who made Heaven and Earth. The structure of the text is exactly that of the Psalm verses, without elaboration, moralizing, or comment of any kind.

The second type is a development of the first. The Lutheran Church based its doctrine on the Bible, and relied, for the spreading of that doctrine among its congregations, upon simple vernacular chorales, many of which were either translations of earlier Latin originals, or what the Scottish Church calls metrical psalms. Some of these chorales were shaped like the old-fashioned morning-songs written by the *Meistersänger* of the late Middle Ages; Nicolai, in particular, produced two of the finest of these: *Wie schön leuchtet der Morgenstern*, and *Wachet auf!*. The secular morning-song had usually concerned two lovers parting at the break of day, with a garrulous and sententious watchman moralizing over their predicament. Here, again, we see the interplay of sacred and secular. The watchman becomes the herald of Christ's coming; the morning-star, Christ himself. Not all the chorales were cast in this form, of course. It is interesting that of all the chorale verses used in

Bach's cantata texts, the largest number dates from the early Reformation period. The combination of biblical verses and chorale verses was therefore a natural and obvious one. The two best examples of this type of text are Cantatas 106, *Gottes Zeit ist die allerbeste Zeit*, and 131, *Aus der Tiefe rufe, Herr, ich zu dir*. In each case, a biblical verse is amplified by a chorale verse sung in conjunction with it. Cantata 106 is a simple sermon on the omniscience of God, set out as a tiny dramatic scena entirely drawn from divers biblical sources. The text—that whatever happens is God's will—is immediately followed by a prayer from Psalm 90: 'So teach us to number our days: that we may apply our hearts to wisdom.' The answer, by the bass (and we shall see that Bach always uses this voice when he is representing God or Christ speaking) is that man must set his house in order, for all men are mortal. The reaction to this is an anxious call upon our Lord to come, followed by a committal of the spirit into God's hands, which draws forth the re-assurance: 'today thou shalt be with me in Paradise'. It is at this point that the chorale verse 'Mit Fried und Freud ich fahr dahin', from Luther's paraphrase of the *Nunc dimittis*, is introduced. The soul is re-assured, and can look forward to dying in the certainty that death is only a sleep. A choral doxology (verse 7 of Adam Reusner's hymn 'In dich hab ich gehoffet, Herr' written in 1533) closes the work.

A further development of these first two classes of cantata consists of biblical text, *plus* chorale verses, and with a few strophes of original verse added. An example of this kind of text is Cantata 71, composed for a council election in Mühlhausen in 1708. The only newly-written elements here are the text of one aria and that of the final chorus; all the rest is taken from the Bible, with the exception of one chorale verse—taken from Johann Heermann's 'O Gott, du frommer Gott' (1630).

A number of Bach's cantatas were composed to old chorales, taken over either completely unaltered, or else slightly modified. Examples of these are *Christ lag in Todesbanden* (BG 4; text by Luther), *In allen meinen Taten* (BG 97, text by Paul Fleming), *Nun danket alle Gott* (text by Rinckart; BG 192), and others. One of the most interesting of these texts is BG 140, *Wachet auf!* which is based on Nicolai's chorale of the same name, but the elements which have been added to the original completely change its nature. The entire chorale is embodied in this text, but to it the librettist has added elements of a miniature operatic scena. It is the custom to regard Bach as an 'untheatrical' composer, implying that he was too exalted a composer to indulge in cheap dramatic effects. Indeed, even so great an authority as Professor Schering, in the preface to the Eulenburg miniature score of this work, suggests that the music contains none of the idea of the watchman shouting to the wedding-guests that they should prepare themselves for the bridegroom's arrival. A more detailed consideration of this text and Bach's treatment of it will be given later on.

Finally, we have those texts composed specially as cantatas; many of these are more or less skilful adaptations of earlier hymns and religious verses; Neumann's[3] handbook includes no less than forty-four of these. Others are completely original, and it is towards these that our attention must now turn.

Towards the end of the seventeenth century, certain writers began systematizing the verse and textual forms used for liturgical purposes in cantatas. Chief amongst these was the schoolmaster and civil servant's son Erdmann Neumeister, several of whose texts were set by Bach. It would not be an exaggeration to call Neumeister one of the important minor figures of baroque literature, since the changes he wrought in the cantata altered its whole aspect. These changes, incidentally, show once more that the fertilization of sacred forms by secular elements was still a living thing at the end of the baroque age.

Neumeister was born at Üchtritz, near Weissenfels, on May 12th, 1671, so that he would have been a student at Leipzig University (where he matriculated in the Theological Faculty in 1689) during the period when the works of the writers of the Second Silesian school were published. In 1695, he became Magister Legens at the University, and submitted his doctoral dissertation on the theme: *De poetis Germanicis huius saeculi praecipuis Dissertatio compendaria*. It was, according to a detailed critical account[4], the first attempt at an entirely aesthetic critical appreciation of poetry ever to appear in Germany, and shows Neumeister's independence of outlook, epigrammatic style, and sharply-focused vision to be indicative of what was to come in German criticism, to culminate in the work of Lessing. The dissertation was very popular, and was reprinted. His other works included *Zugang zum Gnadenstuhl Jesu Christi* ('Access to Christ's Throne of Grace'), published in 1705, which went through twenty editions before Neumeister's death in 1756, and a volume called *Die Allerneueste Art zur reinen und galanten Poesie zu gelangen* ('The most up-to-date method of writing pure and elegant verse'), published without either his knowledge or his consent by C. F. Hunold in 1707. His career as a Lutheran minister took him to Bebra in Thuringia in 1696; in 1704 he became Dean, and later court preacher to Duke Johann Georg von Weissenfels, as well as tutor to his daughter, was called to Sorau as Consistory Councillor and Superintendent in 1706, and, after vigorously attacking the strongly-entrenched pietist faction there in satirical poems, left Sorau for Hamburg in 1715, becoming Pastor Primarius at the St Jakobskirche there.

Ein Heuchel-Volck,

am Hamburgischen

Buß-Tage,

den 18. September, 1738.

aus

Eſa. XXIX. 13, 14, 15, 16,

in einer Predigt

gezeiget,

Und, auf Begehren, im Druck
wiederholet,

von

Erdmann Neumeiſtern.

GOtt der HErr iſt Sonne und Schild.

Hamburg,

Gedruckt und zu haben bey Rudolph Beneke, auf
St. Jacobi Kirchhof.

Title page of a volume of Neumeister's sermons.

Some five of Bach's settings of Neumeister's poems have come down to us. The texts themselves were published in four annual cycles, in 1704, 1708, 1711, and 1714 respectively. The settings that we have are of one from the 1711 cycle, and four from that of 1714. They are:

Gleich wie der Regen (BG 18),
Nun komm, der Heiden Heiland (BG 61),
Wer mich liebet, der wird mein Wort Halten (BG 59),
Gottlob! nun geht das Jahr zu Ende (BG 28), and
Ein ungefärbt Gemüte (BG 24)

An inspection of the last-mentioned of these texts will serve to show how Neumeister set about his task. The formal layout is simple—aria *a* + expository recitative, chorus to biblical text, followed by antithetical recitative *b* + summarizing aria. The plan then, is thesis, hinge-text, antithesis, and closing chorale. The first composite pair, the thesis, as it were, consists of an aria and recitative on the theme of sincerity. The aria speaks of a clean conscience as appearing good both to God and men; all Christian actions should be on this footing. The following eighteen-line recitative, carefully built up of lines of varying length, starts with an assertion that integrity (*Redlichkeit*, which occupies the whole first line) is a gift of God; the counter-assertion, in the seventeen-line recitative after the chorus, is that hypocrisy (*Die*

Heuchelei) is of Satan. The whole of this latter recitative is replete with *Sein-und-Schein* allusions—devils seem to look like angels, wolves are dressed in sheep's clothing, the world is full of slander; God protect the believer from it! The answer to this is contained in the following aria, set, as was the recitative extolling integrity, for tenor voice: Let truth and faithfulness be the basis of all you think, say, and do, and you will be like God and His angels. The closing chorale, a prayer that this may in fact be so, is verse 1 of Johann Heermann's *O Gott, du frommer Gott* (which is also quoted in Cantatas 45 and 71).

It is a feature of those Neumeister texts which have been preserved in Bach's settings that they are all markedly optimistic in tone; the opening line of BG 28—'Praise be to God, the old year is ending'— would certainly have inspired a mid-seventeenth century poet (Gryphius, for example) to count the many miseries of the previous year and to regard the new year as merely another milestone on the way to death. In Neumeister's case, it is a call to count God's blessings, and to thank Him in advance for the good things and further blessings which will be received at His hands during the year to come. That Neumeister was still capable of viewing life in the same manner as the pessimistic baroque poets can, however, be seen from a text of his, not, as far as we know, set by Bach, written for the twenty-fourth Sunday after

Trinity. The Gospel for that Sunday is the story of the raising of Jairus' daughter, and it inspires Neumeister to typically baroque meditation on the transitoriness of earthly things, the certainty of death, and the vanity of earthly life. The images—life as a plaything of vanity, the illusory nature of natural beauties (first of all of the four seasons, and then of the four elements)—aim at showing that all is vanity, which is seen as the result of sin[5]. The lines which were apparently intended for the second recitative begin with an enumeration of four abstracts, all shown to be transitory, and each given an appropriate symbol:

> *Das Eisen frisst der Rost:*
> *Und Stärcke muss zerbrechen.*
> *Die Rosen will ein Käfer stechen:*
> *Und Schönheit ist der Würmer Kost.*
> *Der höchste Turm stürtzt ein:*
> *Und hohe Würde wird nicht frey vom Falle seyn.*
> *Der Sonnen Glantz scheint ohne Flecken nicht:*
> *Und aller Weisheit Licht*
> *Ist dennoch unvollkommen[6].*

The whole of this long passage is baroque, not merely in its method—that of long enumerations, carefully selected and balanced in tension—but also in the images employed and the sentiments they express. Death is the end of all earthly things—but, the poet concludes, it too is an illusion; it *seems* to be the end, but is actually the gate to Eternity. Therefore it is to be welcomed, as the closing aria indicates.

Bach's other principal church cantata text-writers were Salomon Franck (1659–1725), who wrote the texts of most of his Weimar cantatas, and is known to have been responsible for numbers 31, 70, 72, 80a, 132, 147, 152, 155, 161, 162, 163, 164, 165, 168, 185, and 186, and probably responsible for those of numbers 12, 21, and 182; Mariane von Ziegler (1695–1760), who is known to have written the texts of numbers 68, 74, 87, 103, and 128, and is thought to have been responsible for numbers 6, 17, 37, 39, 42, 44, 67, 78, 79, 86, 89, 102, 144, and 166; and Christian Friedrich Henrici, usually known under his pen-name of Picander. Picander is known to have written the texts of Cantatas 145, 149, 156, 157, 159, 171, 174, and 188, and is putatively responsible for numbers 2, 3, 26, 32, 57, 73, 84, 109, 120, 148, and 244a. He was born in 1700 and died in 1764. A number of other writers, such as the two Leipzig pastors, Christian Weiss, Sr. and Jr., are known to have contributed texts to Bach, but the above-mentioned four are those responsible for most of the texts we can attribute to a definite author.

Salomon Franck was a civil servant by profession. After completing his education at the Gymnasium at Weimar, he matriculated in October 1677 at the University of Jena. When his father died, in 1682, he proceeded to Leipzig, in order to study law at the university there, and published a book of religious verse in 1685. On finishing his studies, he went to Zwickau and, in 1689, he was appointed Government Secretary to the Court at Arnstadt. In 1697 he became Consistorial Secretary at Jena, and in the same year published a collection of madrigal-verse on the Passion, entitled *Madrigalische Seelen-Lust*. He remained at Weimar till his death.

In Franck's texts, we find a number of echoes of earlier writers, so definite that one cannot escape the conclusion that he was well-read in baroque authors. He seems to have admired not only their methods, but also their actual turns of phrase. For instance, in the first recitative in BG 72, *Alles nur nach Gottes Willen*, there is a passage distinctly reminiscent of a well-known poem by Hoffmanswaldau[7] :

Herr, so du willt, so muss sich alles fügen!
Herr, so du willt, so kannst du mich vergnügen!
Herr, so du willt, verschwindet meine Pein!
Herr, so du willt, werd ich gesund und rein!
Herr, so du willt, wird Traurigkeit zur Freude!
Herr, so du willt, find ich auf Dornen Weide!
Herr, so du willt, werd ich einst selig sein!
Herr, so du willt,—lass mich dies Wort im Glauben fassen
                    Und meine Seele stillen!—
Herr, so du willt, so sterb ich nicht,
                    Ob Leib und Leben mich verlassen,
Wenn mir dein Geist dies Wort ins Herze spricht!

The rhetorical repetitions of this passage are very similar to those of the poem beginning 'Mund,

der die Seelen kann durch Lust zusammen hetzen,'
which is quoted in a number of anthologies of
Baroque verse[8]. It is the pattern of the poem, with
its effect of a kind of secular Litany, which seems to
have attracted Franck; the form of the recitative is
an adaptation of the sonnet form, as is the Hoffmanns-
waldau poem, and the *pointe* lies in the condition set
forth in the last line. Other evidence of Franck's
literary sympathies can be found in the opening aria of
the cantata BG 168, *Tue Rechnung, Donnerwort*, which
is clearly modelled on the first verse of Johann Rist's
chorale *O Ewigkeit, du Donnerwort*, (itself the basis of
two cantatas), and in the last couplet of the bass
recitative in BG 155, *Mein Gott, wie lang', ach lange*,
which echoes Paul Fleming.

Franck's texts are usually somewhat didactic in
tone. They show enterprise and variety in the choice
of rhythm, and often contain interesting images
inspired by the Gospel text: the aria 'Lass mein Herz
die Münze sein', with its unusual likening of the
human heart to a coin, which occurs in BG 163, *Nur
Jedem das Seine*, is one such example. Indeed, images
concerning money seem to have occurred readily
to Franck, as there is an aria in BG 168 which
begins:[9]

> *Kapital und Interessen,*
> *Meine Schulden gross und klein*
> *Müssen einst verrechnet sein.*

The parable of the unjust steward seems to have inspired this text. A similar image is found in the first recitative of BG 185, *Barmherziges Herze der ewigen Liebe*, where performing acts of Christian love is likened to amassing capital, on which God will pay a rich dividend later—a modernized application of the Gospel reassurance that 'as ye mete, so shall it be measured unto you' in this particular case.

Franck's usual method seems to be to take up various aspects of a text, embroider it, and sum them up in an aria; on occasion, however, he introduces an element of dramatic interplay; in BG 152, 172, and 21 (if he wrote it) there are dialogues between the Saviour and the soul, culminating in a kind of mystic union between the two. The terminology is in each case that of a love duet, with the female partner, the soul, seeking out the male (the Saviour, or, in the case of BG 172, the Holy Spirit).

Mariane von Ziegler was married three times; the first of these was in 1711, when she was 16, to Heinrich Levin von Könitz, who died in 1712. Her second husband, G. F. von Ziegler, whom she married in 1715, died in 1722, and she returned to live with her mother in Leipzig, where she made the acquaintance of the literary reformer Gottsched in 1724. She published her first poems, *Versuch in gebundener Schreib-Art* ('An Essay in a strict Style') in two parts in 1728 and 1729. Two years after the appearance of the second part, she was elected to the *Deutsche Gesellschaft* in Leipzig, of which Gottsched was the President. In 1733, the University of Wittenberg elected her Poeta Laureata, and she was chosen as poetess to the Emperor. In 1739, having published her *Vermischte Schriften in gebundener und ungebundener Rede* ('Miscellaneous Writings in strict and free form'), she met W. Balthasar Adolf von Steinwehr, who had become secretary of the Gesellschaft in 1738, and was elected Professor of Philosophy at the University of Göttingen in 1739. They were married in 1741; this time her husband was considerate enough not to leave her a widow, and she published no more poetry before her death in 1760.

A comparison of the texts of the two cantatas named *Wer mich liebet, der wird mein Wort halten* (BG 59 and 74, respectively), is instructive, since one is by Neumeister, and the other by Ziegler; music from his earlier work is used by Bach in the later. Both works begin with a chorus to the words of St John's Gospel, Chapter 14, verse 23, which is the first verse of the Gospel for the day. The divergences begin with the second number. In Neumeister, it lays emphasis on the great honour that the message of this gospel constitutes for the body of believers; the unworthiness of man, who is as dust, the plaything of sorrow and misery, is then commented upon. Throughout, the plural pronoun is used—it is as a collective that the congregation is viewed. There follows the chorale verse: 'Komm, heiliger Geist, Herre Gott' (from Luther), and a closing aria commenting on the fortunate state of the blessed ones who know that they have God in their hearts—and saying how much more blessed they will be when they in their turn leave Earth to go and live with God in Heaven.

In Ziegler's text, the second number is an aria— an invocation *by the individual* to the Saviour, who is invited to come and take up His dwelling in the heart of one who loves Him. The emphasis is completely personal, and Neumeister's original (the closing aria from BG 59) has been thoroughly reworked. The following recitative repeats the invocation more concisely, and is answered by a bass aria, taken from the same part of the Gospel as the text of the opening chorus: 'I go away, and come again unto you. If ye loved me, ye would rejoice.' This is followed by a tenor aria calling upon all to rejoice because, although the Saviour is going away, He will return. A short recitative reassures those who are in Christ that there is no condemnation for them (Romans viii. 1), and is followed by an aria acknowledging that only Christ's blood can save them from the chains of Hell. The cantata closes with a chorale verse (verse 2, from Gerhardt's *Gott, Vater, sende deinen Geist*) which states that no man is worthy of this great gift, which has been achieved by Christ's atonement. Ziegler has quickened up the quasi-dramatic action of the original in two ways; firstly by changing the whole from a general, collective action to a single, individual one, and secondly by bringing the appeal to the Saviour into second place in the text from third, cutting out the rhetorical exegesis contained in Neumeister's first recitative, and drastically reorientating his closing aria.

The relationship of the texts to individual characters—that is to say the emphasis on the individual and particular rather than the general and communal relevance of their message—is a marked feature of all those texts of Ziegler's which have come down to us in Bach settings. The participants sing of their *individual* joys and fears; the texts are less impersonal, less didactic. Though the participants cannot be called characters in a dramatic action in our sense of the term, they are nonetheless something of a step in that direction compared to their counterparts in Neumeister's texts.

Picander was born at Stolpen, near Meissen, on January 14th, 1700, where he was educated. From here he went on to the University of Wittenberg, and published a series of occasional poems, mostly satirical, in 1721. His sarcastic wit—which was later put to use on Bach's behalf in *Phoebus and Pan*—won him enemies, and in 1724 he adopted safer—i.e. sacred — themes, publishing a number of cycles of cantatas.

He was, of course, also responsible for the texts of the St John and St Matthew Passions. His work was widely read in Leipzig, and went into four editions between the original date of publication and 1748. Like Franck, he was a civil servant—an exciseman— and makes humorous reference to his livelihood in the *Peasant Cantata* (BG 212). He seems to have been Bach's favourite librettist, as he was entrusted, not only with the two passion texts, but also with most of the *pièces d'occasion* which Bach was called upon to provide for birthdays, Royal occasions, and so on. Like Franck, he was capable of illustrating a biblical text with a topical allusion. In one case, he actually uses a commercial image—that of a bill—referring to our Lord's death:

> *Ich habe meine Quitting hier*
> *Mit Jesu Blut und Wunden unterschrieben*[10].

Baroque images and metaphors are to be found in most of his texts.

In most of the texts that have come down to us, the 'sermon' is quite simply built up, and its relevance expounded either to the congregation at large or to the individual believers of which that congregation was composed, in the shape of argument and counter-argument. There are, however, a number of texts which go much further than this; the quasi-allegorical interpretation of scripture is extended into a quasi-dramatic one. This is done in one of two ways.

Either some scriptural event is narrated, taken out of its historical setting, and topically related to the present congregation as a parable or allegory, or else it is actually turned into a miniature drama, played out in the soul of the believer. I have already mentioned BG 140, *Wachet auf!* This cantata is one of the most interesting examples of the latter type. Unfortunately, we do not know who adapted Nicolai's magnificent hymn. The expansion takes the form of an insertion, between verses 1 and 2, of an excited recitative with images drawn largely from the Song of Solomon, ending with the words: 'See ye; lo, He comes!' A duet follows between the soul and the Saviour, with an extremely elaborate violin figuration, closing with a yearning request by the former to open the wedding-chamber for the heavenly meal—i.e. Communion, which is recognized as one form of mystic union with the Godhead. The second verse of the chorale follows, and is succeeded in turn by a bass recitative (clearly expressing the Saviour's sentiments) imploring the soul to enter and submit to His love. This is received with rapture in a duet, and the whole congregation joins in rejoicing afterwards.

The whole atmosphere of the text is one of super-charged excitement and elation, often couched in highly erotic terminology; the chorus represents the wise virgins in the first instance; the tenor is the narrator—or, if one will, the watchman. But the central characters are Christ and His bride. Viewed in this light, Schering's assertions that the music of the first chorus contains no theatrical effect, and that the rhythmic pulsation of the violins has nothing to do with watchman's signals seem a false compliment to Bach's understanding of it. It is strange indeed, if Schering's account is correct, that the only time the theme first heard on the violins

is taken up by the voices, it is to the words 'Allelujah' and 'Macht euch *bereit*'. Moreover, the *tessitura* of the voices lies for the most part rather high, the orchestral accompaniment simply bursts with rhythm, and the word 'Wo?' is constantly repeated. Is it not likely that Bach saw this text as a small-scale mystical drama, and was deliberately aiming at underlining the dramatic elements in it?

The text of BG 60, *O Ewigkeit, du Donnerwort*, is based on Johann Rist's chorale of that name, of which another setting (BG 20) also exists. The latter text is simply a close adaptation of Rist's grim conducted tour of Eternity for the damned; BG 60, on the other hand, is quite different. The impersonal warning of Rist's first verse is used as a starting-point for a much more gentle interpretation of the poem. Rist's treatment of the theme is assumed to be inspired by fear, and the Cantata is worked out in terms of an antithetical dialogue between Fear and Hope. Whereas BG 20 is didactic, impersonal, and minatory, BG 60 is resigned, hopeful, personal, and submissive. Fear is shown in the process of being vanquished by Hope, and she has an answer to all his claims, showing misgivings towards all his optimism, save the last. Not even the text, 'Blessed are they which die in the Lord', is enough to comfort her, until the words 'From henceforth' are added. Here is the decisive *occasio* which brings her round to his point of view. The trick, so common in baroque drama, of removing a spiritual or existential obstacle only to find another in the way, is here repeated no less than nine times before the struggle is resolved. The contrast is underlined between fear of eternity and patient waiting upon God. Bach even enhances the dramatic effect at this point at the beginning of the last duet-recitative, Fear saying:

> *Der Tod bleibt doch der menschlichen Natur verhasst*
> *Und reisset fast*
> *Die Hoffnung ganz zu Boden*[11].

She is answered, not by the tenor voice of Hope, but by the bass, with the voice of the Scriptures. And at the end, after the conversion has been accomplished, she says:

> *So stelle dich, o Hoffnung, wieder ein!*

It appears that Bach noticed this; hence his use of another voice for the vital text.

The text of Cantata BG 32, *Liebster Jesu, mein Verlangen* is an excellent example both of the process described above and of the topical allegorizing of historical scriptural events. Like the two texts just discussed, it contains a dialogue, in this case, once more, between Jesus and the soul. The Gospel for the Sunday in question is the story of the twelve-year-old Christ being lost in the Temple, and His parents' anxious search for Him. In the first aria, the soprano voice represents not only His mother, but, at the same time, the lost individual soul. Just as Mary had lost contact with Christ's person, physically, so the soul loses contact spiritually; both ideas are embodied in this text, and it works on two planes at once. Jesus, in the guise of the bass voice, answers in a recitative from the Gospel narrative and an aria developing it in more general terms, and the action is continued in a dialogue recitative followed by a duet, in which the soul is enjoined to abandon earthly things for God; this done, the pair rejoice, and the final chorale is a prayer that all may do likewise.

Other examples of this, but without the duets, can be found in BG 154 (*Mein liebster Jesus ist verloren*), BG 81 (*Jesus schläft, was soll ich hoffen?*), and BG 82 (*Ich habe genug*). In each of these cases, a factual scriptural narrative is interpreted in allegorical terms and related to the topical needs of the individual believer. BG 154, like BG 32, derives from the Gospel story of the child Christ in the Temple, and the subject is treated in much the same way as it is there; BG 81 concerns the story of the storm on the Sea of Galilee, and Christ's stilling of it. Here again, an actual event is given an allegorical interpretation—the favourite baroque theme of life as a sea-voyage came naturally to the librettist's mind—and after the uncertainties and discomforts of a stormy voyage, with Belial's waves curling round the ship, all is set right by a word from the Saviour. Clearly, the bass aria 'Schweig, aufgetürmtes Meer!' derived as it is from Christ's own words as recorded in the Gospel, is envisaged as delivered by Christ—otherwise, why the possessive pronoun in '*mein* auserwähltes Kind' and the subsequent alto recitative beginning 'Wohl mir, mein Jesus spricht ein Wort'?

Perhaps the most interesting example of this pro-cess is the text of BG 82, one of Bach's two solo cantatas for bass voice. It is usually thought that the singer for whom this great work was written was a student; whoever it was must have had a magnificent voice. The Gospel from which it is derived is the story of the presentation of the infant Christ in the Temple, and the reaction of the old man Simeon. As will be remembered, the theme of Simeon's song is 'Lord, now lettest thou thy servant depart in peace, *for mine eyes have seen thy salvation.*' That is to say, the old man wishes to die because the purpose of his life has been fulfilled. This is the burden of the first aria in the text, and the bass soloist embodies both Simeon's joy at seeing the Saviour, and that of the contemporary believer who knows of the certainty of his faith. This is driven home in the subsequent recitative, which, however, introduces a new thought: if only I, too, could say good-bye to this world. It is important to note that the reason given for the 'death-wish' here is quite different from Simeon's. The baroque Christian finds the world a vale of tears, and wishes to leave it as soon as possible; it is of no significance for his soul:

> *Welt, ich bleibe nicht mehr hier,*[12]
> *Hab ich doch kein Teil an dir,*
> *Das der Seele könnte taugen.*

So runs the text of the aria 'Schlummert ein'. The recitative which leads from that aria to the finale, 'Ich freue mich auf meinen Tod' refers not only to the death-wish, but also to the beautiful *moment* ('das schöne *Nun!*') when the individual will be translated from this world into the next—a typically baroque sentiment. So, by an argument which is not unlike a series of puns, we reach the conclusion—I long for my death, too. As Simeon is *willing* to die, now that the purpose of his life has been fulfilled, so the baroque Christian *wishes* to die—because life is a burden to him.

Sometimes the dramatic element, instead of being allegorized, is combined with didactic warnings. This is the case in BG 46, *Schauet doch und sehet*, which, like *Wachet auf!*, is a miniature operatic scena. It divides naturally into two parts. The first chorus, with a text from Lamentations i.12, represents the citizens of Jerusalem bewailing the coming destruction of their city. Their cries are rebuked by the narrator in the subsequent recitative; because Jerusalem ignored Christ's warning, she shall be destroyed and the following bass aria drives this lesson home. It is possible that the bass here represents Christ giving judgment on the unfortunate city, or it may simply be that Bach wanted the darker colour of the bass voice for the remorseless text. With this aria, the first part of the action, such as it is, comes to a close.

The didactic commentary now begins. The thesis of the argument is delivered by the alto: do not imagine that Jerusalem is the only city under threat of destruction—it can happen to you, too. The antithesis follows immediately in an alto aria: even so, Christ will stand by those who believe in Him, and the cantata closes with a prayer for mercy.

What is interesting in all these examples is the combination of baroque allegory and motifs—such as the world as a vale of tears; life as a sea voyage; the necessity for remaining steadfast in adversity; suspicion of worldly goods and good fortune (neither of which is necessarily regarded as a mark of God's favour: see, e.g. the aria 'Man nehme sich in Acht', in BG 166); the 'vanitas vanitatum' theme of a world full of illusion (sometimes in reverse, as it were, as in the first recitative of BG 161)—with pietist elements, such as inner drama and sudden conversion after a dark night of the soul, within an orthodox Lutheran theological framework and baroque Lutheran scholastic interpretation of scripture. We should be surprised neither at this nor at the quasi-dramatic nature of some of the texts. Neumeister himself felt it necessary to define the cantata —both sacred and secular—as the smallest musico-dramatic form, and C. F. Hunold defended the 'theatricalization' of sacred material by asserting that it enabled people to realize more vividly and emphatically in their hearts what was known to be spiritually true[13]. The Church Cantata is a rhetorico-dramatic exegesis of a scriptural text, lifted on to the plane of worship by a closing chorale. When we consider the aim and the nature of German baroque drama, we shall see how much more dramatic these works are, in the sense in which the word was understood in Germany in Bach's day, than has up till now been generally realized. Scheibe, indeed, who was no friend of Bach's, and who thought Bach's treatment of his texts far too illustrative and elaborate, actually admitted that although arias and choruses should be kept within the bounds of strict form, the recitative, which carried the burden of the dramatic action, should be full of fire, élan, and emphasis[14].

We should do well to remember that a good deal of the 'dramatic' element in German baroque tragedy was dependent on rhetoric and on the thrust and counter-thrust of argument. Moreover, the chorus, which was an important element in the baroque play, changed its function and character from act to act; allegorical and dramatic action sometimes intermingled. Because this is the case in these works, because they require no scenery, and because the same soloist can be active as a Biblical character, a commentator, or an individual soul crying out for salvation within the course of the same cantata, we need not assume that the dramatic element does not exist. Moreover, the text of any cantata ought to be read as a rhetorical or dramatic unity, not simply as a collection of odd observations strung together for no very good reason. That such collections exist among Bach's texts is undoubtedly true—but there are also a good many texts which, by the standards of the early eighteenth century, have aesthetic values of their own based on canons which have unfortunately long since ceased to have much meaning for us. Some of those canons may have been demonstrated in the

Johann Mattheson

Erdmann Neumeister

present chapter; I hope to give some idea of others of them when considering the texts of Bach's secular cantatas, which are, in their own way, of just as much interest as works of baroque literature.

III. THE SECULAR CANTATAS

If one reads—a laborious enough task in all con
science—one of the verse tragedies of such a write
as Jakob Bidermann, Andreas Gryphius, or Danie
Caspar von Lohenstein, one is struck by the differ
ence between what German baroque writers made
out of Senecan recipes and what our own Eliza
bethans created from a similar source. For wherea
both are apt to engage in bombast, moralizing, and
crudities, the English writers seem to be much more
interested in the creation of living individual char
acters, whether or not these are symbols of some
greater, more abstract conception. Some of the more
likely reasons for this have already been given in the
first chapter.

One of the features of baroque drama in Germany
taken over from the Dutch by Gryphius, and retained
for other reasons by Lohenstein, was the chorus. A
the end of the act, the main characters retired from
the stage, the *kleine Welt* of human activity, and
group of symbolic characters stepped forward and
took their place. These characters might represent
the seasons, or a group of virtues, or even geogra
phical features, such as rivers. Their purpose varied
from writer to writer and from play to play. In

54

Gryphius, they usually fire off a moral broadside aimed at the audience; in Lohenstein, they sometimes develop the basic political, moral, or emotional issues inherent in the action of the spectacle which the audience has just witnessed, and sometimes lift the play out of the particular and historical into the realm of the topical by relating its action to a contemporary personage.

These solemn choruses, which were often laid out in the shape of an elaborate baroque ode, with argument and counter-argument, offered an excuse for spectacular masque-elements, and possibly a form of ballet. It seems certain that in the Jesuit dramas they were accompanied by music[1]; it is known that this was probably the case in the Dutch plays, and it appears quite likely that this was so with Gryphius, if not Lohenstein. That such spectacles were not unknown in England is shown by the existence of Purcell's *Fairy Queen*, an enormously elaborate allegorical masque tacked on to the end of the various acts of a truncated version of Shakespeare's *Midsummer Night's Dream*, rather more, I suspect, for spectacular than for dramatic reasons.

It is no surprise, then, to find that themes developed by Lohenstein in his *Reyen*, as these choruses were called, were also taken up by Bach's librettists as the basis of some of his secular cantatas. I make no claim that Lohenstein directly influenced, say, Picander, when the latter chose the story of Hercules at the Crossroads, or a chorus of rivers as bases for cantatas, for the former theme, at any rate, derived via Seneca from Sophocles. But it is plain what has happened here. What had, in baroque drama, been a symbolic interpretation of a dramatic event—the same event played out on an ideological level—was now detached from its parent body so that it led an independent existence of its own, having become a form instead of an appendage.

Moreover, the choice of subject for the *Reyen* was sometimes conditioned by the intention of the play. In Lohenstein's *Sophonisbe*, for example, the symbolic drama of *Hercules at the Crossroads* appears at the end of the fourth act, and is explicitly stated to be a parable of the youth of the Emperor Leopold. The masque itself is a projection of a dream experienced by Masinissa, Sophonisbe's husband, who has, in the play, been confronted with the choice between a virtuous but inexpedient course of action and a vicious but expedient one. For Masinissa, the reward of virtue will be the recovery of his throne; for Leopold, it will be a happy and prosperous reign. The second purpose here is clearly to link the action of the drama itself to contemporary events; to show that in the Holy Roman Empire of the seventeenth century such intrigue, bloodshed, and violence could not possibly happen, because the ruler of that Empire had made *his* choice correctly, unlike Masinissa. The choruses of rivers which occur in Lohenstein's *Epicharis* and *Cleopatra* serve the same end. In Gryphius, this was not the case, the main characters in the play being presented as paragons of stoic virtue anyway (save in the one case of his first play, *Leo Armenius*) and there was thus no need for the *occasio* outside the action of the play itself. In Lohenstein, the whole business is a matter of *contrasting* the stability ensuing under the reign of a virtuous prince with the chaos endemic in a world dominated by Fortune, self-interest, and the debased form of stoicism where characters control their passions in order to hide their true motives from their scheming underlings and unreliable allies. In the independent secular cantata, the contrast cannot of course be drawn; implied, indirect praise is replaced by explicit, direct flattery.

The process of separating the *Reyen* from the main body of the play did not occur suddenly at the end of the seventeenth century, however. In addition to the solemn baroque verse tragedies of Gryphius, and Lohenstein's supercharged versions of the Gryphian model, there were other types of drama performed both at seventeenth-century courts and in the towns. One of the most interesting of these from our present point of view was the *Festspiel*. It should not be thought that Bach's secular cantatas were a kind of poor bourgeois substitute for the elaborate spectacle provided for the court in the Opera. Quite apart from the fact that there was a celebrated Opera at Dresden, there was also an operatic theatre in Leipzig itself[2]. Yet these theatres between them did not exhaust the possibilities for musical drama. As Professor Flemming points out[3], it was not so much a matter of a poorer public desiring a less expensive form of musical spectacle that engendered the *Festspiel*, but an intellectual desire. Opera as performed in seventeenth-century Germany was sensuous, exotic, and extravagant; in a number of places it was sung in Italian to music composed by Italian immigrants. In the opera it was usual to portray the sudden changes of Fortune which were customary in baroque drama, but moralizing on them (usually in arias) was part of the action itself, not left over to a detached chorus of allegorical figures at the end of each act. The mythological abstractions embodied in that part of baroque drama went over, via the *Festspiel*, into the Cantata, which was neither a substitute for opera nor a forerunner of it, but a separate development from the same root. The cantatas were frequently performed by night in the open air[4], and there seems to be no good reason why they should not have been acted as well as sung.

The *Festspiel* may possibly have been a baroque development of the *Fasnacht* plays and moralities of the sixteenth century; it certainly went as far back as the allegorical and didactic plays by the Hamburg pastor Johann Rist, whose name we have already met in connection with Bach's Church Cantatas. Four of these plays survive, and they all contain the double stage, which appears to have been introduced into Germany by the first professional actors ever to appear there, early in the seventeenth-century— the groups of travelling English actors known as the *Englische Komödianten*. This double stage had an inner area curtained off, and was very simply furnished. Little scenery was required, and it is unlikely that there was a backcloth. Such furniture as was found on the stage might fulfil a symbolic function (such as would be the case with a throne, representing authority, a couch, etc.)

Music was an important element in these plays, as indeed it must have been in most baroque drama. Gryphius calls for incidental music in *Leo Armenius* and *Cardenio und Celinde*—even going so far as to specify that it should be provided by viols—in order to heighten the mystery and tension of some scenes. Rist actually wrote[5]

What sort of a pitiful situation would exist in tragedies and comedies if no moving music accompanied them, of such a nature as to invest such plays with their true life and grace, so to speak?

Opportunities were provided for angel choruses and

strophic solo songs, accompanied either by the solo-ist himself or by hidden instrumentalists, a procedure of which Richard Wagner would have approved, and which Rist himself explicitly preferred! One sus-pects that Rist himself felt that drama without music was certain to be rather dull—the statement quoted above almost admits as much—possibly because of its didactic aim and sententious nature. Moreover, at the end of each act, there was an orchestral ritornello—as had been the case with the *Wanderbühne*—and in some cases music accompanied the spoken word. The arrival of princely personages was heralded by a fanfare. But the music was still secondary to the action of the spoken text.

In some of the seventeenth-century *Festspiele*, such as Schottel's *Friedens Sieg* (1642; first published 1648) there were pastoral interludes which formed a *Sing-spiel*. Andreas Gryphius, too, wrote a play in which idealized and popular elements were combined—his *Die geliebte Dornrose*—in which a pastoral *Singspiel* and a dialect drama not unlike parts of Bach's *Peasant Cantata* alternated, scene for scene. In the world of opera there was a distinct division, by the end of the seventeenth century, between *opera seria* and *opera buffa*, though comic characters were still to be found in serious libretti—a parallel to which may be noted in the comic elements in the heroic baroque novel, such as Scandor in Ziegler's *Die Asiatische Banise*. For example, in Postel's libretto to *Gensericus*, a heroic opera about the Vandal King, there is a comic servant, called Turpino, whose manner of behaviour harks back to lighter baroque writers such as Greflinger on the one hand, and foreshadows Schickaneder's Papageno on the other. *Gensericus* was performed in Hamburg in 1693, and is well endowed with baroque spectacles, such as processions, banquets, and so on. It is worth noting that the favourite baroque tags, about constancy in love, firmness in the face of adversity, the blows of Fortune and the glories of a simple life, are all to be found in this libretto. Why they were there can perhaps be seen from the following passage, taken from the writings of the early eighteenth-century librettist Feind[6]:

The end of the first act must proceed to complete confusion, and the characters must be so involved with one another that neither the spectator nor the reader is able to guess the poet's intention.

In other words, the paraphernalia of baroque drama were to be retained—such as the constant *Glückswechsel* and complex action—but for quite a different reason. Gryphius introduced such things into his dramas because he was convinced that the world was like that; his peripeteia were underlaid by a metaphysical system of beliefs and a philosophy that enabled him at least in theory to surmount Fortune's challenge. Feind retains the outward form of the baroque dramas, but introduces these elements as a technical device to confuse, stimulate, and entertain the spectator. Professor Flemming points out that happenings in Feind's own libretti are markedly similar in some places to those in Lohenstein's *Sophonisbe*.

How baroque tags and images persisted in the operatic libretti can be seen from this quotation—again taken from Postel's *Gensericus*:

> *Ein Felsen-gleicher Helden-Muth*
> *Spielt mit des Donners-krachen*
> *Er schertzet in der Flammen Wuth*
> *Kan bey dem Schiffbruch lachen*[7].

Here, there are a number of baroque images—'Felsen-gleich' reflects the stock image for a constant stoic, showing a firm front to the world. A hundred years later, the same image was to be used—in quite a different context—by the Abbate da Ponte, in *Così fan tutte*, when Fiordiligi claims that she will remain faithful to her beloved, come what may. It is an obvious image, and it is certainly not merely a baroque one, but in the seventeenth century, 'rock-like' nearly always implied a stoic attitude. 'Er schertzet in der Flammen Wuth' is here intended to be taken quite literally, as is the image of the shipwreck in line 4; there are numerous examples of both tags in baroque literature, but they are almost invariably images, metaphors rather than just word-pictures. Moreover, in the recitative following this aria, there is a reference to constancy, and in the quartet preceding it, an invocation of *das Glück;* in this case, we are not to understand the capricious and often malicious force of baroque poetry and drama, but positive good fortune and material blessings.

No wonder, then, that Fortune herself appears in some of Bach's secular texts, and the word *Glück* itself, sometimes devoid of any allegorical significance, recurs on a number of occasions. It seems nearly always to mean positive, material good fortune. How different from, for example, Lohenstein!

The Cantatas themselves seem to fall into three categories, with one, the *Coffee Cantata*, cheerfully and obstinately refusing to be categorized. Of the quasi-dramatic ones, there are those written to 'prove' something, such as *Phoebus and Pan*, or *Hercules at the Crossroads*, and there are those written in honour of someone (to which class *Hercules at the Crossroads* also belongs), such as *Der Zufriedengestellte Aeolus*, *Was mir behagt*, or the *Peasant Cantata*. All of these have some remote—in some cases some very remote—resemblance to a present-day drama about them, mixed in with a good deal of sententiousness and flattery. The third type of Cantata consists of the quasi-philosophical discourse, such as *Ich bin in mir vergnügt*, or *Weichet nur, betrübte Schatten*.

The first thing that one notices about these texts is the reckless bandying about of the names of classical divinities; it does not seem to matter to Bach's librettists whether they are called by their Greek names or by their Roman, and of course little thought was given to the matter, simply because they were not there to act as personalities—save perhaps in the exceptional case of *Phoebus and Pan*, which was Picander's rude riposte to Scheibe's sarcastic criticisms of the former's friend—Bach. When these classical gods take part in a dramatic action in the cantatas, they are not expected to follow the accepted plan of a known legend in every case. In *Was mir behagt*, for example, Diana and Endymion appear, together with Pan and Pales. It is true that Endymion complains that Diana has been showing him too few favours of late, but the reason for this is that she has been devoting her attention to the Prince for whom the cantata was written. The reconciliation between her and Endymion takes the form of their joining together in paying homage to the Prince. (It does not matter which one; the cantata was used for two different princes at least.) An interesting feature of this text is that hunting was a recognized leisure occupation of the virtuous ruler—Simon Dach, for example, wrote a poem in honour of a Prussian prince which extols this very activity[8]. A baroque delight in trumping the superlative *may* perhaps be detected in the plot; all the audience would be acquainted with the legend of Diana and her love for

Endymion. Clearly her attraction to the Prince must be a very strong one to entice her away from so handsome a youth! The powers of virtue having paid their homage, it remains but for Pan, and later Pales, the shepherd and shepherdess, to pay theirs. Such little action as there is consists therefore in the reconciliation of Diana and Endymion.

Phoebus and Pan and the *Coffee Cantata* stand on rather a different footing. In the case of the former, the story of the old legend is faithfully followed, but again the action is given a topical twist. Here, the symbolic baroque characterization is modified; things happen, and the characters take on a certain shape and identity. Whereas Diana, in *Was mir behagt*, is a mere embodiment of the virtuous prince's love of the chase, Phoebus is Bach himself, and Midas is Scheibe. And in the *Coffee Cantata*, the tiny drama concerns neither real people dressed up as Roman or Greek gods, nor allegorical personifications of human characteristics, but a grumpy old man and his vivacious daughter. The *Coffee Cantata* and the *Peasant Cantata* are the only two which break tentatively away from the formal baroque tradition and into the different world of more 'realistic' bourgeois drama.

Yet even in the more formally baroque cantatas, we can see that the atmosphere is different from that of the models. This is perhaps best demonstrated by comparing Lohenstein's text of *Hercules at the*

Crossroads to Picander's, which was published some forty years later, at a time when Lohenstein was still a living influence in parts of Germany[9], though many critics approached his works with their noses in the air.

There are, to begin with, a number of points of similarity. First of all, of course, we have the fact that Hercules is a symbol for a prince whom the Cantata was intended to flatter, just as Lohenstein's *Reyen* are meant to flatter a Holy Roman Emperor. Secondly, in both versions, there is a certain amount of imagery based on flower-symbolism. Thus, in Picander we find the lines:

> *Die Anmut gehet schon voran*[10]
> *Die Rosen vor dir auszubreiten;*

a perfunctory enough reference. In Lohenstein, however, the reference is to chrysanthemums, and the symbol is taken up and expanded in the next couplet (in both cases, the flowers are offered by *die Wollust*), because Virtue points out that they are full of wasps. There is no such expansion in Picander; the image is simply, and weakly, discarded. The same is true of the reference to snakes—which also occurs in both versions. In Lohenstein the picture is carefully built into an antithetical series of enumerations; in Picander it is casually and inconsequently introduced into the second part of an aria.

In Lohenstein's version, for all its floweriness and exaggeration, there is a certain amount of rhetorical dialectic; the fact soon becomes apparent that *Tugend* (Virtue) is being identified with *Sein* (Reality), and *Wollust* (Lust, or Delight) with *Schein* (Illusion), and that the two antagonists are engaged in a skilfully constructed debate, where they outbid one another in pointing out the flaws in their respective arguments. In Picander, there is none of this; the outcome is known from the beginning—has not the Council of Gods declared in the opening chorus that it will look after Hercules? The struggle is therefore quite artificial, and it is thus significant that Hercules' choice is made, not from an inner decision, but after consulting an echo-oracle which automatically gives him the correct answer. In Lohenstein, *Wollust* gives ground inch by inch, stage by stage in the argument; in Picander, she simply disappears from the scene halfway through the cantata. There is no dialectical struggle, no baroque superlative-trumping, no *Sein und Schein*. The baroque forms have been retained, but the purpose behind them has been completely abandoned; outright and optimistic flattery has replaced a rhetorical tension and an implied flattery. Moreover, the way in which Picander uses such words as *Ruhe* and *Lust*[11] differs markedly from the way in which a seventeenth-century poet would use them. We must look elsewhere than in the libretto of this cantata if we would find truly fundamentally baroque elements. All that we have here is the convention of the virtuous prince and the fact that the *occasio* underlying the work lies outside its actual action.

Such is also the case with *Der Zufriedengestellte Aeolus*, which was written not for a prince, but for August Müller, Professor of Philosophy at Leipzig University, in 1725. Here, the legend of Aeolus unleashing the winds is made the *occasio* for a flattering allusion to the fact that he is prepared to call them in again on hearing that it is Professor Müller's birthday. The legend states that Aeolus lets the winds out at autumn so that they will destroy what is left over from summer and thus prepare the way for winter. The fact that Professor Müller's name was August(us), and that his birthday was in that month, doubtless aided Picander in his choice of subject. Müller himself is *not* Aeolus, but it is on his account that Aeolus recalls the winds he has released. It is typical of the whole nature of baroque exaggeration and flattery to imply that the course of the seasons can be checked on account of a mere provincial Professor of Philosophy's birthday. As in *Hercules at the Crossroads*, therefore, the *pointe* of the action lies outside the characters directly involved in it. On this occasion, the issue is not quite the same as in the later cantata, however; Hercules is a *symbol* of the person honoured and flattered, whereas here (as in *Was mir behagt*), the dedicatee influences the action from outside, as it were.

Some baroque literary motifs of Bach's day

left:
Frontispiece to Ziegler's *Täglicher Schau-Platz der Zeit*, third edition, published in 1728, the year before the first performance of the *St. Matthew Passion*

right:
Frontispiece to Glaubitz' *Die Anmuthige Pistophile*, published 1713

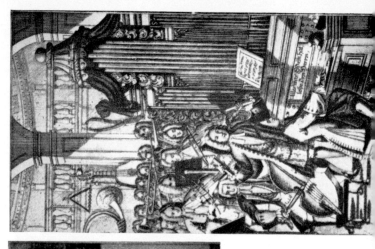

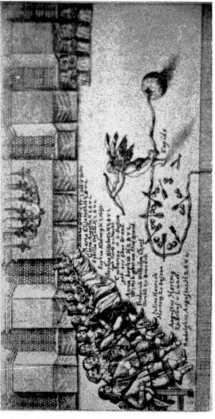

Two performances of the Baroque era

Above: A secular *Festspiel* performed in costume in a banqueting room before a distinguished audience.

Right: A sacred cantata performed in a church.

The solo secular cantatas descend more from the baroque ode than from the choruses in baroque drama. Here, there is no *occasio*[12]; simply, as in many of the Church cantatas, something in the nature of a musical sermon. Only here, of course, the issues are philosophical rather than religious. Echoes of baroque stoicism are to be found in BG 204, *Ich bin in mir vergnügt*, which is a cheerful and optimistic treatment of a theme well known in the seventeenth century, and BG 202, *Weichet nur, betrübte Schatten*. The former is really an ode in praise of stoic self-sufficiency, and the latter seems to have been a wedding-cantata of some kind, with the two partners considered as virtuous lovers of the kind well known in seventeenth-century novels such as Zesen's and wedding-epigrams, such as those of Logau (1604-55). As such, they hardly differ, save in their marked optimism, from many such verses written in the seventeenth century; they regard virtuous self-sufficiency and a virtuous marriage respectively as a barrier against the assaults of mutability, and as a positive gift of good fortune and material welfare in a rather difficult world, but there is little of the sense of anxiety and apprehension that is to be found in similar poems written seventy-five years earlier. Once again, the conventions are observed, but the basic premisses underlying them are but shadows of their former selves.

It is quite clear from certain early eighteenth-

F

century theoretical works that the cantata was regarded as the smallest-scale musico-dramatic form of the period. Neumeister[13] stated that after the opera came a number of other forms and with typically German thoroughness he described and defined each genre in turn. The *Serenata* was a one-act musical drama. It need not, he remarked, be always performed on the stage, but could be done without scenery as a *Tafel-musik*. He also mentioned what he called an *Operetta*, and ,'if a ballet or an *entrée* is danced after each scene', the whole work was called, he said, a *Ballet*. If, however, princely personages and other people of rank were involved, wearing costumes as participants, then it was called a *Masquerade*—of which he gave, as an example, a *Singspiel* with four characters and a chorus. A *Pastorale*, he observed, is analagous to an opera and a serenata, in that it is smaller than the former, but larger than the latter, though similar to both. The smallest form of all mentioned by him was the cantata itself, which 'has the appearance of a part of an opera'. He further laid considerable emphasis on the importance of pastoral characters, whilst admitting that 'hunters, gardeners, and deities, etc.' could be included. The fact that the two first-mentioned are included as stock features presumably derives ultimately from the fact that in the seventeenth century both hunting (see above) and the garden (see, for example, Beyerlinck's *Theatrum*

vitae humanae and Part II of Lipsius's *De Constantia*)
were regarded as conducive to stoic virtue; it was
occasionally a feature of baroque drama to include
gardeners in the chorus (as Lohenstein does, for
example, in *Ibrahim Sultan*). The usage prevailed,
though the stoic underlay had been forgotten by the
end of the seventeenth century. Lohenstein's gardeners are envied by those in high positions, but not
because of their stoic virtue; rather is it because of
their lowly position in life and therefore their freedom from the dilemma of having to make decisions.
Even in Lohenstein, then, the true nature of the
symbolism has been obscured; by the time we reach
Picander, it has become a mere counter in a rather
conventional literary game.

All these elements point backwards at the old
baroque drama; the writers took over its constitu-
ents without always understanding what lay behind
them. A more forward-looking development can perhaps be seen in *Phoebus and Pan*, the *Peasant Cantata*,
and, above all, in the *Coffee Cantata*. For here, instead
of allegorical conventions, we have real people, however sketchily drawn; instead of *occasiones*, we have
real happenings and topical satire; instead of for-
malism, a certain realism. Except in the case of the
Peasant Cantata, the element of a flattering tribute to
authority is entirely missing from these three works;
the interest lies elsewhere—in the development of a

situation in terms of character interplay. Even in the *Peasant Cantata*, this feature is to a certain extent present.

It is not difficult to expound the action of any of these pieces. Such action as there is is simple and devoid of surprises, *Glückswechsel*, or any other of the paraphernalia of baroque drama. In the *Coffee Cantata*, Lieschen incurs her father's wrath by drinking too much coffee; he overcomes her craving by refusing her a husband. But she gets the better of him by making the secret reservation—a feature which Bach himself appears to have added to Picander's original text—that she will accept no suitor suggested by her father unless he permits her to make as much coffee as she pleases. (It could, I suppose, be argued that this new element, as introduced by Bach into Picander's original poem, is evidence of his 'baroque' mentality in that it trumps Schlendrian's superlative, but it seems to me that this is rather a slender argument—though not the only one—which seems to suggest that Bach's mind did work in a similar manner to that of the truly baroque artists.) In *Phoebus and Pan*, the tension develops between the characters, and the dénouement in the unfortunate Midas' fate. (The fact, by the way, that Mercury refers to Midas' receiving a fool's cap, in the aria 'Aufgeblasne Hitze' may well indicate that here, at any rate, enough props were required to warrant at least one non-musical scenic action—the placing of the cap on Midas' head to represent his asses' ears.) In both these cases the usual moralizing is inserted at the end of the dramatic action.

The *Peasant Cantata* is an act of homage of rather a different kind from the other cantatas of this type, in that instead of idealizing the dedicatee as a paragon of all virtues, defender of his country, and so on, the position is reversed; both the 'hero' and his wife— who, of course, stand outside the action of the drama —are 'one of us'; the landlord knows as well as his tenants how pleasant it is to flirt—which a princely hero would never be assumed to do. His wife is in no way proud—'a good egg'; she doesn't talk down to her tenants; she is thrifty, and virtuous in the sense that bourgeois and peasants understand the term rather than scholars and courtiers. That is to say, her virtue lies in her practical management of the everyday affairs of life, not in any idealized subscribing to a philosophic code of conduct. There is, moreover, a recurrence of the theme taken up in *Phoebus and Pan*, in that the bass Bärenhäuter (translated in the Eulenburg score as 'old gorilliar', in order to rhyme with 'familiar'!) sings a naïve aria—the music is that of Pan's aria from *Phoebus and Pan*—which is regarded as too rude for the elegant city folk.

Clearly Bach's librettists, living as they did in an age of transition between two styles, betrayed elements of both; the old, sententious baroque drama is here mixed with the first glimmerings of the newer middle-class drama that later developed into the comedies and tragedies of Lessing. It is notable that the type of dramatic action is quite different, depending on the public for which it was intended and to the purpose for which the cantata in question was written. The cantatas were not intended for repertory performances, as operas of the period undoubtedly were, but that does not mean that they were not envisaged as small-scale dramas. It is easy enough for us nowadays to see the dramatic elements, such as they are, in *Phoebus and Pan*, or in the *Coffee Cantata;* what is perhaps not so simple for us is to envisage what is regarded as dramatic in the libretti of the other cantatas. The solo cantatas we can disregard; where there is simple lyric exposition and theorizing by one character, there will be little or no drama. But in the others, the dramatic element consists principally in the fact that a philosophic *occasio* is presented in terms of allegorical characters, as had been the case in the *Reyen* of baroque drama. As Professor Flemming points out[14], these allegorical characters were never meant to have any personal reality or identity, even in the seventeenth century. Mars, he says, was not the God Ares, but an embodiment of the abstract concept War. The dramatic value, therefore, lay not in the appearance of such a character *per se*, but in its associations—the drama was something intellectually experienced at one remove from what was actually seen. That is why the legends and myths were so blithely adapted, related to topical situations, and recast. The purpose of such plays—particularly of the *Festspiele*, and even more of the *Reyen* at the end of each act of a baroque tragedy, lay not in the play and interplay of character and situation, but in the presentation in concrete symbolic terms of moral, political, or philosophical issues.

In this particular sense, then, these cantata texts can be regarded as small-scale dramas—certainly in the sense in which *Festspiele* and *Reyen* were works of drama. It should not surprise us that the same poet, Picander, should be capable of writing both types; the public for whom he wrote differed quite markedly from work to work. A text for a *Tafel-musik* for the worthy citizens of Leipzig was somewhat different in aim and method from one designed to flatter a prince or a don. Nor should it surprise us that baroque motifs are sprinkled over the texts without much consideration of their relevance. Traditions die hard, even today in the twentieth century, and the old writers were not yet forgotten, even though their works were subject to some criticism. Yet it is an interesting reflection that the *Peasant Cantata* was written some seven years before the birth of the greatest of all German poets.

IV. BACH AND HIS TEXTS

I have mentioned allegory and symbolism a good deal when discussing Bach's cantata texts, pointing out that they were an important element in baroque German literature. It would, however, be rather a wan argument, even if it were not a false syllogism, to state, as if it were self-evident: 'Baroque writers used allegories; Bach used allegories. Therefore Bach was baroque.' Musical allegory and symbolism is something of quite a different nature from verbal and dramatic allegory. Yet, I believe, there is a certain parallel to be drawn between the two arts, and it can be shown with a fair amount of confidence—not more, for the evidence is not strong enough to support anything more than a conjecture—that Bach was a 'baroque' composer in other senses as well as those now accepted.

In the last chapter, it was pointed out that much of the 'dramatic' nature of baroque *Singspiel* and the cantatas which in part descended from it depended on allegory. Dramatic allegory is simple to achieve. It consists in taking a well-known characteristic of human life and presenting it as a person, giving it opinions to express and comments to make. Thus anyone playing the part of Fortuna would be allotted lines which seemed to the poet to express the attitude of mind that he felt motivated her actions. In the seventeenth century, she was regarded simply as a spiteful agency who allowed people to prosper only to cast them down suddenly; that was her sole delight in existence, and the higher they rose, the more delight she took in bringing them down. In Lohenstein's dramas, to give one example, she becomes articulate unpredictability. In his *Cleopatra*, for instance, she is acknowledged as queen of all the gods, and Jupiter, Neptune, Apollo, Mars, and Mercury all pay homage to her and hand over their sceptres. In this, Lohenstein was simply stating that power, the elements, manliness, heroism, and so on, were all subject to the mutability of an unpredictable world. Again, in *Epicharis*, she is depicted as engaged in a struggle with Raison d'état, Time, and Fate concerning what shall happen to Nero; the final decision, made by all four together, is that they shall combine forces and destroy Nero's Rome. This is simply a personified and spectacular way of saying that it was neither expedient, nor fated, nor timely, that such a corrupt and amoral state should survive.

Thus in Bach's cantata texts, verbal allegory might consist of the personification of religious concepts— such as the Holy Spirit, or the soul, or it might consist in taking a biblical event, known to have happened once and for all in history, and applying it

as a topical generalization to the present congregation. It might, in the secular cantatas, consist in
personifying the just ruler's virtuous passion for
hunting by disguising it as the Roman goddess Diana.
But whatever the case, a theory was virtually placed
on a stage and treated as a character, without being
expected to have any human identity.

Musical allegory, on the other hand, cannot work
in this way. There are a number of methods in which
it can be used—a simple example, of course, is the
ascending scale which often accompanies the words
'Et ascendit' in settings of the Mass. But once a
pattern of this kind is put into a musical movement,
the design of the movement often determines the
function of the motif. An example of this is the first
chorus of BG8: *Liebster Gott, wann werd' ich sterben.*
According to Schering, the orchestral background
accompaniment represents the bells of Leipzig, as
they were wont to toll at funeral services; the bass
sounds on the first and seventh beats of a 12-8 bar;
the violins play pizzicato arpeggios, and the flute in-
tones rapid, quivering, repeated semiquavers on the
same note. The peal apparently consisted of five
bells[1], the highest of which was very shrill, and
gave a rapid tinkle when a funeral service was to take
place. There seems to be no reason why Schering's
conjecture should not be correct; what is important
to notice, however, is that the allegorical association

(tinkling bell—death) which is associated with the text of the movement, forms the basis of the complete musical design of this first chorus. Its use and development is dictated entirely by the shape of the musical form—a large-scale chorale fantasia.

This, however, is not the only form of musical allegorization used by Bach. On a smaller scale, we have the illustrations of words which are so common in his elaborate arias and sometimes in recitatives. This is achieved in a number of different ways.

Studies by Manfred Bukofzer[2], and Arnold Schmitz[3] have discussed Bach's use of symbolism in music in considerable detail; they have shown that his choice of certain melodic and harmonic turns of phrase is often used by association to illustrate the meaning of the words. And although this interpretation of musical symbolism can be carried too far, as Walter Emery has pointed out[4], there can be no doubt that such symbolism was the standard practice in certain types of music in the early eighteenth century. Schmitz's study was based on consultation of a number of works of baroque theory published at various times in the seventeenth and eighteenth centuries. That Bach himself was criticized rather severely on occasion for attempting to illustrate the words too closely in some of his works is clear from accounts by Scheibe quoted by Schmitz. Indeed, Scheibe even went so far as to compare Bach to Lohenstein, and he certainly did not mean it as a compliment[5]. This surely indicates that Bach's whole technical apparatus was regarded in some quarters as out-of-date for the same reason as Lohenstein's was: the cast of mind underlying the prodigious technical ability was unsympathetic to certain early eighteenth-century theorists. It would be the simplest thing in the world to say that Scheibe represents the early *Aufklärung*, and that he was reacting against the baroque style—simple, and misleading. And yet it would not be totally wrong to do so.

A study of the relationship between words and music in the Bach cantatas, both sacred and secular, along the lines undertaken by Schmitz and Bukofzer (who devote considerably more attention to the former than the latter) shows that Bach's treatment of key-words in arias was quite similar in both cases. The 'musical symbolism' falls into a number of distinct categories. The first of these is simple pictorialism, where the ear is called upon to aid the inner eye. Words like 'waves', 'snake', 'arrow', 'ladder', and so on, are variously illustrated by this method, as the following examples indicate:

The fact that Ex. 2 comes in a recitative, where the text is set one note for each syllable in the overwhelming majority of cases, strengthens the claim that this is illustrative of the arrow's flight. Ex. 3 can be parallelled in a number of cases from other cantatas, both sacred and secular, such as e.g. the second movement of Cantata 92, or the second movement of Cantata 207a *Auf, schmetternde Töne.*

A parallel method is that of 'illustrating' abstract concepts by images which are not exactly pictorial, but suggest the visual aspect of the abstract concerned. The joyous association of a word like *jauchzen* (to rejoice) is, for example, illustrated by a repeated jump of a sixth:

the shining and shimmering associations of *glänzen* (to gleam), and its related noun *der Glanz*, by an elaborate

melisma (see, e.g. Cantatas 173a-vii, 213-vii), or the
flickering aspect of the word *Flamme* (flame) by a
similar device (BG 208-iii, BG 207-vii,) to which we
may add the treatment of the word *Feuer* (fire) as for
example in Cantata 34-i.

We can already see that a roulade of semiquavers
was used to denote the associations of a number of
words quite different in meaning, and that therefore a
type of phrase cannot be said to be a 'motif' of something. A musical pattern cannot be said to *mean* anything extra-musical by itself, but *in conjunction with its
text* an emotional association developed which col-
oured the significance of a particular musical phrase.
In an article in the *Journal of the Warburg Institute*[6],
Bukofzer quotes an example from the second section
of an aria better known as 'Bereite dich, Zion', from
the *Christmas Oratorio*, which was originally set to a
text in *Hercules at the Crossroads* and intended to be
associated with deceptive snakes lulling the hero into
a complacent stupor. In the sacred text, the words
run:

> *Deine Wangen*
> *Müssen heut viel schöner prangen*[7]

which, in addition to providing exactly the same
combination of final syllables as the original (*Schlangen*
—snakes, and *fangen*,—catch or trap) for purposes of
euphony, can also be 'illustrated' by an identical
musical phrase without spoiling the associative effect.

There is another interesting example of this kind of transference in the same pair of works—in the Arias 'Auf meinen Flügeln sollst du schweben' and 'Ich will nur dir zu Ehren leben'. In the secular text, the roulade exactly fits the associations of *schweben* ('hover', 'float'):

The sacred text has *leben* ('live') instead—and fits far less suitably as an association, though again the vowel and consonant scheme is exactly the same. It is the music, not the association, that is of primary importance; but that does not mean that the melisma in question was not intended to work illustratively by association in the first place.

A further form of melodic illustration by association is that which Bach seems frequently to use in the case of verbs. Elaborate figuration, as in the case of *schweben*, mentioned above, or in the following:

is one of the methods he employs; sequence—particularly in the case of verbs such as *führen* (to lead) and *bauen* (to build)—is another, as the next example shows:

Examples of this sequential treatment of phrases set to one of these words can also be found in BG 39-i, to the word *führen*, and in the first movement of BG 56, to the phrase *der führet mich*. On the other hand, words like *ruhen*, and their derivative abstract nouns and adjectives, which obviously imply lack of motion, he usually illustrated in the simplest possible manner by just putting down a long held note for the duration of the word, while the remaining parts move against it. Since all motion is relative, this obvious and natural device is one of the most effective methods of associative illustration. It is used in setting the words *Bleib bei uns*, for example, in the second, fugal section of the first chorus of BG 6, for *Ruhe* in BG 19-iii, for *schläft* in BG 81-i, for *Schlaf* in BG 161-iv, for *ruh'n* in BG 176-ii, and perhaps the most interesting example of all (the others are, of course, by no means exhaustive, but taken more or less at random)—the following, from BG 204. As has been stated, this cantata is a eulogy of stoic self-contentment, and the

opening recitative is instructed to be sung over a long
held pedal B flat:

Ex 9 (BG 204-i)

Ich bin in mir ver-gnügt. Ein an-drer ma-che Grillen, er wird doch nicht da-mit den Sack noch Ma-gen fühlen

In Chapter I, it was pointed out that '*Die Ruhe des
Gemüts*' meant, for the stoic, more or less what is
defined in this cantata. I believe that the pedal note
here is an allusion to *Ruhe* (there would be less point
in its being an allusion to *Schlaf*, or any of the other
words mentioned above!), for the harmonies implicit
in the vocal line above it change quite colourfully. It
should be remembered, too, that this is a recitative,
not an aria, and that the words themselves are treated
with the normal syllabic recitative declamation.

The above devices are all primarily melodic; when
we come to consider harmonic and rhythmic illustrations of words, we find, much as we would expect
in a composer whose work is architecturally built on

G

key-structure, that chromaticism and dissonance imply disturbance of some kind. This does not mean, simply because Bach was in the habit of so setting words like *Jammer* (misery) *Schmerz* (pain), and so on, in this way, that any occurrence of such passages in his wordless works may be considered to be necessarily illustrative of these emotions, and should therefore be performed with an excess of plangent sentiment. But it can mean that his use of dissonance and chromaticism is not always purely architectonic. It is the duty of the performer to decide which is the more likely interpretation of such a passage by a careful study of the nature of the work and the musical and verbal context. A whole-tone passage:

may be used, for example, to give the idea of darkness; a semitonal sequence

to imply misery; a long-drawn chromatic melisma to show torture:

Such turns of phrase occur quite frequently. Just as the words to which they are set imply that a normal harmonious state is disturbed, so the manner of setting them disturbs the flow and harmony of the musical impact.

This usage extends further. The following example is taken from the opening chorus of *Bleib bei uns* (BG 6), and in it, the gathering darkness of approaching evening is simply and effectively symbolized by the chromatic vagaries of the theme:

On occasion, Bach even goes so far—a parallel this to the case already mentioned above regarding the first chorus of *Liebster Gott, wann werd' ich sterben*—as to build up the rhythmic bass of a whole aria on a phrase probably designed to illustrate the word 'net':

Again, the motif itself may or may not have an illustrative function, but its overall use in the movement
is determined on musical grounds alone. But this
factor does, nonetheless, have an important bearing
on the interpretation of certain movements. I have
already (see above, p. 45) pointed out how the
association of a phrase (heard mainly in the orchestra)
with a particular line of a chorale in a chorale fantasia movement may well determine the whole aspect
of the movement, and therefore of the manner in
which it is meant to be interpreted. It is always
useful for the conductor of one of these works to
study not only the musical texture, but the association between music and words; this is usually
revealing, and sometimes gives a valuable clue to the
choice of tempo, etc.

A feature which is sometimes melodically, sometimes rhythmically, and sometimes harmonically
managed is the forcing of the vocal or instrumental
line for the sake of pictorial effect—particularly in
the case of verbs which imply energetic motion or
activity. Sometimes this is just lightly attractive—as
in the case of Diana's first aria in *Was mir behagt*,
where the word *jagen* (to hunt) is set to an arpeggio
figure in 6/8 time and the 'a' vowel is declaimed
staccato on each note—clearly in imitation of a
hunting horn. Sometimes it is adopted for satirical
reasons—as is the case with the word *wackelt*

(wobbles) in Pan's aria in *Phoebus and Pan*:

—a phrase which is used in exactly the same comic way, a deliberately clumsy way, in the aria 'Dein Wachstum sei feste' in the *Peasant Cantata*, only this time rather more appropriately to the word *lachen* (laugh). (Even so, the performer would do well to bear in mind what is said in the next recitative about this aria—that it is not really suitable for the refined taste of the sophisticated city-dwellers who were among the audience.) Sometimes, however, the illustration is pictorial, representing perhaps the play of the elements:

Here, the height of the roofs is (possibly) illustrated by the octave jump on the first syllable of *Dächer*, and the cracking as they fall in the insistent little rhythmic figure *a* in the first violin accompaniment, as well as the voice part.

Rhythmic figures used as repeated motifs in recitatives or ariosi seem in many cases to take their point of departure from certain key-concepts in the text. In the aria 'Ätzet dieses Angedenken' (BG 207-viii) the violins and violas, in unison, play the motif:

piano sempre against a flowing accompaniment on the flutes. The likely explanation here is that the insistent rhythm was suggested by the word *ätzet* (etch), and that the text is here being, as it were, 'contrapuntally' treated—one thought being insistently borne in upon the listener, while the other thoughts expressed in the text vary somewhat. Again, in the duet-recitative 'Augustus' Wohl ist der treuen Sachsen Wohlergehn' in *Auf, schmetternde Töne*, the little motif:

might quite easily represent Augustus' power, which is the insistent theme of the text here. This is reminiscent of the little rhythmic 'growl', expressly marked *con pompa* in the opening recitative of the *Coffee Cantata*, which clearly marks the advent of Lieschen's father, Schlendrian—as Drinker suggests in the Eulenburg score, 'Old Stick-in-the-mud' might be a good English translation.

The most elaborate examples of this 'contra-puntal' symbolism occur, of course, as Bukofzer points out, in the church cantatas, when a chorale melody is quoted on an instrument against an inde-pendent voice part in an aria or chorus. Examples of this come readily to mind, such as in the first aria of *Komm, du süsse Todesstunde* (BG 161), where *Herzlich tut mich verlangen* is quoted, or in the aria 'Letzte Stunde, brich herein', from *Der Himmel lacht*, where the violin and viola play the chorale melody *Wenn mein Stündlein vorhanden ist* against an oboe obbligato, or in 'Sei getreu', in *Weinen, Klagen*, where a trumpet plays the melody of *Jesu meine Freude*. The melody is meant, as Bukofzer says, to stand for itself as a musical element in the structure and at the same time, to evoke the words to which it is usually set. The congregation would presumably recognize the tune, and associate it with the appropriate words, though those words themselves would not actually be heard. This is a rather complex symbolism. Two trains of thought are intended to be set up in the listener's mind—those of the actual words he hears, and those of the unquoted words of the chorale, which often contrast with or add to the significance of the actual text as sung. Here, then, we have the double effect of two simultaneous emotional reactions, and the fact that they are both musically expressed by associa-tion. Bukofzer himself gives an even more elaborate example from *Du sollst Gott, deinen Herren, lieben*, where the chorale melody, *Dies sind die heil'gen zehn Gebot*, is played on the trumpet against the text 'Du sollst Gott, deinen Herren, lieben' while the bass of the chorus takes up the trumpet melody in canon, and in augmentation. Bukofzer draws attention to other allegorical features of this music. At once, the difficulty arises concerning a contemporary performance in England as to how much of all this symbolism would be readily understood by the audience. Only very few chorale melodies are at all well known to us, and any allusions to their tune may not mean anything to anyone save those well versed in German religious poetry and music. The critic is left in the rather unenviable position of the learned professor explaining all the details of an elaborate humorous anecdote if he is compelled to point out all the allusions. But some form of explanation is necessary, especially for the performers, because such questions as choice of tempo and intensity of delivery are so often bound up with the sentiments expressed in a certain line of the text set. For the rest, the allusions must regrettably, but necessarily, be regarded as largely lost, and the audience's concentration centred on the purely musical structure.

These devices are not programmatic; indeed, programmatic music of the onomatopoeic type (cuckoo-calls, etc.) was regarded as a rather primitive form of musical symbolism in the early eighteenth century. Mattheson[8] even considered it superficial, because it only imitated sounds rather than making implicit any deeper content. The phrases were intended to make their pictorial or emotional impact by association of ideas, which was thus delivered in two stages, *via* an intellectual process, using the conventional musical symbolism of the age. Mattheson writes[9]:

Many people will think from the above that we have now been employing such things and figures for so long without knowing what they mean or what they are called that we may abandon them and discard rhetoric. These people appear to me to be even more ridiculous than Molière's *bourgeois gentilhomme*, who had previously had no idea that it was a pronoun when he said: 'I, you, he', or that it was an imperative when he said 'Come here!' to his lackey.

This is evidence enough that these figures—like the faded images and allegories of late baroque literature —were regarded by many as clichés and counters. Yet knowledge of them was vital to the learned baroque composer. Kuhnau, a predecessor of Bach's at St Thomas's, Leipzig, emphasized that the composer should not only be able 'to move the affections and to express all such things skilfully', but also 'to understand the right sense and scope of the text all the time', as well as being well versed in scriptural exegesis[10].

Bach himself left no hints as to what he regarded as good and suitable use of allusive figures, nor did any of his pupils say what his method was. This is understandable, even if regrettable, as German taste in both music and literature was even in his own day reacting against the baroque. It is only known that he did teach his pupils to take good note of the effects implied in the text[11]—an opinion in which even Scheibe concurred.

Schmitz devotes a good deal of attention to the extremely elaborate catalogues and explanations of rhetorical musical devices which are to be found in early eighteenth-century manuals, but since these devices all worked by association, and since the association by which they worked is now all but lost to us, it is merely interesting, and not vitally important to know them. A text was inspiring to a baroque composer in so far as it contained allusions which could be worked out in terms of such figures. Thus we have the assertion made by Mattheson that even feeble, dry texts can form the basis of rich musical invention *because of their allusions* rather than their beauty[12]. It is essential to remember that neither for the baroque poet, nor for the baroque composer, was the sensuous or lyric value of a text of any importance, nor yet its direct emotional impact, but its sententious and didactic value, or its *Scharfsinnigkeit*.

We can perhaps gain some idea of the form reactions to Bach's music took if we compare the elaborate B minor aria for Phoebus in *Phoebus and Pan* to Pan's own aria later. Phoebus' is marked *Largo*, with an elaborate orchestral ritornello and accompaniment, with all the dynamics carefully marked in; words like *zart* (tender), *verlangen* (desire), *hold* (sacred), *Morgensterne* (stars of the morning), and *der Seelen Sonne* (sun of the soul)—all affective words— are drawn out in melismas. Pan's aria—and Midas', too—is much simpler in its figuration *though completely in Bach's style;* fewer, and less 'affective' words are elaborated, such as *wackelt* (see above, p. 89), *Tanze* (dance) and *Scherz* (joke). The criticisms—if this aria can be accepted as being of the type that Scheibe liked—seem to us irrelevant, because the treatment is merely a rather simpler variant on the same baroque theme. Like the attempts at reform instigated by literary critics like Gottsched, during the same period, these attacks were made on baroque music by people who still, to a certain extent, based their attitude to art on baroque theory and practice. Drama still meant sententious rhetoric—even if it also meant less feverishly active heroes and less Senecan rant. A beautiful text meant an allusive one, and a good setting of it, one which followed up different allusions—and not so elaborately as Bach did.

We have already seen how the cantata and the

opera developed along rather different but parallel lines out of the sententious baroque drama and *Festspiel;* we have seen that the cantata was regarded as a small-scale dramatic form. Many of Bach's texts were in fact called *Dramma per musica*, and he must surely have been conscious of what to him were dramatic elements in them. A composer who could write something as rhetorical as the opening movement of the second part of the St Matthew Passion, and who could handle harmonic relationships in recitative so vividly as he, was surely neither bound to the organ-loft nor so other-worldly and anti-theatrical as is usually assumed. Unlike Handel's, however, Bach's ideas of dramatic usage were those of seventeenth-century Germany, and not that of eighteenth-century Italy, or England. The dramatic elements in his cantatas are the rhetorical and allusive ones rather than the personal, save perhaps in the *Coffee Cantata* where, significantly enough, he successfully portrays character. Choruses in the secular cantatas usually consist not of people, but of virtues, winds, rivers, and so on. and are therefore allegorical. It is, paradoxically enough, in the church cantatas that the more conventionally dramatic elements—tension, excitement, suspense—enter the text—and illustration of them is by no means absent from the music. The favourite baroque allegory of *navigatio vitae*, for example, is most strikingly handled in BG 81 (in the aria: 'Die schäumenden Wellen von Belials Bächen') where in a number of places the flow of the music is interrupted by adagio passages to illustrate the Christian standing firm against the onslaught of the waves. In bars 29/30, the voice part breaks into a flourish which derives from the figure played by the violins in the ritornello, as an illustration of the word *verdoppeln* (double—i.e. double their rage), a procedure which recurs in bar 39. At bar 47, there is a sudden *Adagio* 4/4 instead of the *Allegro* 3/8 which is the basic metre of the aria, which recurs in bars 51 and 52/4. In the same cantata, incidentally, the Saviour's injunction to the sea to hold its peace is apparently rather reluctantly obeyed; Bach's desire to illustrate the violence of the sea—as witness the dramatic semiquaver flourishes in octaves on the strings—being evidently stronger than his need to show the sea obeying the command. That he *was* conscious of dramatic implications of this nature can be seen from the famous recitative in the *Kreuzstab* Cantata, where the 'wave' figure in the continuo ceases the moment the text indicates that the Christian has landed from the ship.

But Bach's dramatic sense is not restricted to energetic musical rhetoric in such situations. The love duet in *Wachet Auf!* between Christ and the soul, his bride, is accompanied by an extremely ornate violin obbligato—in some ways resembling that of 'Erbarme dich', in the St Matthew Passion. Here, the expectant emotion is portrayed by the elaborate rhetoric of the melodic line; if this is taken as a good example of the allusive content of an ornate melody, it may well be a clue to the interpretation of such melodies in other contexts. But as I have been at pains to stress above, it is wrong, and dangerous, to assume that a certain type of musical phrase has an extra-musical emotional meaning. And, of course, it is equally wrong to interpret a highly emotional melodic line by imbuing it with all forms of so-called 'expression', inserting extraneous dynamics, excessive vibrato, and all the devices of modern technique. Wrong—but not so reprehensible as some critics would have us believe—for it is substituting direct emotional appeal for emotional appeal *via* intellectual association. Bach's 'sewing-machine counterpoint' is not so poker-faced and inexpressive as some of his latter-day imitators would like to think. But we need not impose upon it the musico-dramatic practices of a later age with quite different ideas about expressing emotion in musical terms.

It should not be forgotten, either, that Bach frequently used music which had been composed to one text in order to fit a different one. This is certainly not evidence that he could not help writing in a sacred style; it merely means that one 'effect' could be used for different purposes. This is somewhat reminiscent of Gryphius's procedure in the two versions of his drama *Carolus Stuardus*. In the first version of the play, Fairfax is one of the villains, and in a stichomythic dialogue scene, he is given the 'bad' lines; in the second (the play having been rewritten after fresh evidence had been revealed about the roles played by the participants in King Charles's trial) the words in this scene that had formerly been put into Fairfax's mouth were given to his antagonist and *vice versa*. No clearer example could be given of the fact that baroque drama was based on entirely different premises from ours—of character and situation development being interdependent. Similarly, because Bach originally wrote the music of the Crucifixus from the B minor Mass to a text laden with rhetorical complaints about the misery of a Christian's lot on earth, it does not necessarily follow that the music illustrates the mystery of the crucifixion from the rhetorical and pathetic angle—Christ murdered—rather than from the mystic or spiritual—the self-immolation of the Godhead to atone for the sins of the world. But it could well mean that a dramatic or rhetorical interpretation of this chorus *might* be nearer Bach's original conception of it than the 'spiritual' one involved in singing it right through *pianissimo*.

That Bach regarded music and text as interdependent is surely shown by the care he takes to adapt allusions inherent in the texts he set; that he did not regard the music as completely subservient to the text can be seen from the fact that he always kept the illustrative elements within bounds and developed the music according to strictly musical laws, never allowing allusion to or illustration of too many words to disrupt either the shape of the musical design or the clarity of emphasis in the arias.

Throughout this chapter I have been at pains to point out how Bach's attitude to the relationship of words to music and his interpretation of his texts was in keeping with the baroque outlook. Certain other traces of the baroque mentality *may*—and I stress the word 'may'—possibly be found in his technical procedure of what could be called the 'broken cadence' —a number of these occur, for example, in the first movement of the A minor violin concerto, and in the first movement of the fifth Brandenburg Concerto. I mean the manner in which a theme is lengthened and the final cadence postponed by a sudden swerve in the direction of the melody. The following example, from the aria 'Adam muss in uns verwesen', will show what I mean:

Ex 19a (expected cadence) *tr* (BG 31 · vi)

b (actual cadence) *tr.*

Is it too far-fetched to see in this procedure a technical parallel to the broken façades which are a recognizable feature of baroque architecture, or the overtrumped superlatives which are a notable part of baroque literature? Both certainly indicate a temper of mind which delighted in the impact of a delayed and unexpected sensation. As Dr. Odette de Morgues has pointed out[13], there is a preference in baroque novels, epics, or pastorals, for ambiguous situations in those works dealing with profane love. She is writing of the beginning of the seventeenth century, yet the temper of mind which delighted in such things did not disappear quickly, even if what had once been a spiritual necessity degenerated into a technical device.

For the rest, it is clear that Bach's procedure in setting words worked largely by association and not by direct illustration; that his texts contained elements which were readily understood as allegorical allusions by his contemporaries, and that his settings are certainly not as 'objective' as has sometimes been assumed. It is above all important to remember that his cantatas, whether sacred or secular, were not just odd collections of rather beautiful arias interspersed with chunks of recitative and other arias somewhat less beautiful. The texts, however sententious and precious they may seem to us today—and many of them quite naturally do—were quite frequently

H

intended to have a certain kind of dramatic unity, a
the term was understood in early eighteenth-century
Germany, whether or not that unity was based on
rhetoric or on allegorizing. A cantata is often a
dramatic suite; both words and music are almost
always there to illustrate and emphasize a central
theme, to reinforce its impact, and to decorate it
That their development takes place in self-contained
movements (which could be removed from their
context and set in other works) rather than a long
continuous movement is not in itself a disadvantage
it merely shows that composers of Bach's day did not
set so much emotional store by their music—it was
true *Gebrauchsmusik*, in fact—as was the case in later
ages. And whilst purely musical consideration
determined the shape of individual movements, rheto
rical ones often determined that of the musical
ornamentation within those movements, and quasi
dramatic ones the shape of the whole cantata. The
division between cantata, concerto, suite and sonata
was not so strongly marked in Bach's day as it has
since become. Operatic, sacred, and instrumental
music were not mutually exclusive, concert life not
nearly so highly organized, orchestras less rigidly
constituted. The crystallization of highly differen
tiated musical forms and the emergence of the artist
prophet rather than the artist-craftsman were yet to
come. We do Bach a disservice if we forget this.

NOTES

CHAPTER I.

1. Martin Opitz, *Das Buch von der teutschen Poeterey*, reprinted in *Neudrucke deutscher Literaturwerke des 16. und 17. Jahrehunderts*, Halle, 1879, p. 24.

2. L. W. Forster, *The Temper of German Seventeenth Century Literature*, London, 1952, to which I am much indebted, gives a concise and stimulating picture of German literature of the baroque period, and a useful short introduction to the lyric of that age in the foreword to his *Penguin Book of German Verse*, London, 1957, pp. xxxiii–iv.

3. Preface to the 1629 edition, pp. 98 ff.

4. Büchner's *Letters*, Dresden, 1679, Vol. I., p. 154.

5. Manfred Bukofzer, *Music in the Baroque Era*, London: J. M. Dent & Sons, 1948, p. 80.

6. Kurt Berger, *Barock und Aufklärung im Geistlichen Lied*, Marburg: Verlag Hermann Rathmann, 1951.

7. See Forster, *Penguin Book of German Verse*, pp. 43–44.

8. H. K. Kettler, *Baroque Tradition in the Literature of the German Enlightenment*, Cambridge: W. Heffer & Sons, 1947, pp. 76–77.

9. Ian Finlay, 'Bach's Secular Cantata Texts', *Music and Letters*, Vol. XXXI, No. 3, pp. 189–95.

10. Kettler, ibid., p. 66.

CHAPTER II.

1. L. F. Tagliavini, *Studie sui testi delle Cantate Cacre di J. S. Bach*, Cassel & Basel: Bärenreiter Verlag, 1956,

p. 45, footnote 1. Tagliavini's book is painstaking and useful, but does not aim at being a work of literary criticism. Its value is almost exclusively documentary.

2. *Grove's Dictionary of Music & Musicians*, fifth edition, ed. Eric Blom, London: Macmillan & Company, 1954, Vol. I, p. 305.

3. Werner Neumann, *Johann Sebastian Bach Sämtliche Kantatentexte*, Leipzig: Breitkopf & Härtel, 1956. An invaluable and thoroughly documented book, carefully indexed and cross-referenced.

4. Sigmund v. Lempicki, *Geschichte der deutschen Literaturwissenschaft bis zum Ende des* 18. *Jahrhunderts*, Göttingen, 1920, p. 175.

5. W. Flemming, *Oratorium und Festspiel*, Volume 6 of the group *Barockdrama* in *Deutsche Literatur in Entwicklungsreihen*, Leipzig: Philipp Reclam Verlag, 1933, pp. 62–64.

6. Flemming, *Orat. & Festsp.*, p. 63. Translation: 'Rust consumes iron, and strength must break in pieces. A beetle will sting roses, and beauty is food for worms. The highest tower collapses, and high dignity is not free from a fall. The sun's brilliance does not shine without blemish, and the light of all wisdom is imperfect, come what may.'

7. Neumann, p. 79. Translation: 'Lord, if thou wilt, everything must go according to plan! Lord, if thou wilt, thou canst grant my request! Lord, if thou wilt, my torment will vanish! Lord, if thou wilt, I shall become healthy and pure! Lord, if thou wilt, sorrow will turn to joy! Lord, if thou wilt, I shall find pasture among thorns! Lord, if thou wilt, I shall be blessed one day! Lord, if thou wilt, let me grasp this word in faith

and content my soul! Lord, if thou wilt, I shall not die, even though my body and life desert me! If thy Spirit speaks this word to my heart!'

8. Hofmann v. Hoffmanswaldau, quoted in Max Wehrli, *Deutsche Barocklyrik*, Basel: Benno Schwabe & Co., 1945, p. 79.

9. Neumann, p. 231. Translation: 'Capital and interest, all my debts, great and small, must be paid one day.'

10. Neumann, p. 126. Translation: 'I have my receipt here, signed in Jesus' blood and wounds.'

11. Neumann, p. 319. Translation: 'Death remains abhorrent to human nature, and quite [probably not 'almost' as it would be today] tears Hope to the ground.'

12. Neumann, p. 334. Translation: 'World, I shall no more remain here. I have, after all, no part with you which could mean anything to my soul.'

13. Flemming, pp. 19–20.

14. Quoted by Flemming, pp. 20–21.

CHAPTER III.

1. See Joseph Ehret, *Das Jesuitentheater zu Freiburg in der Schweiz*, Freiburg im Breisgau: Herder & Co., 1921, pp. 87, 108–10.

2. See Emil Ermatinger, *Deutsche Dichter 1700–1900, Eine Geistesgeschichte in Lebensbildern*, Frauenfeld: Huber Verlag, 1948, Vol. I, p. 37.

3. Flemming, *Orat. & Festsp.*, p. 117.

4. See Arnold Schering, *J. S. Bach's Leipziger Kirchenmusik*, Leipzig: Breitkopf & Härtel, 1936, pp. 118–19.

5. Quoted by Flemming, *Orat. & Festsp.*, p. 129.

6. Quoted by Flemming, in *Die Oper* (Vol. 5 of the same series), p. 24.

7. Flemming, *Die Oper*, p. 231. Translation: 'A hero's courage, rock-like, plays with claps of thunder, jokes in the rage of a fire, and is able to laugh in a shipwreck.'

8. See Simon Dach, *Gedichte*, ed. H. Oesterley, Stuttgart: Bibliothek des Literarischen Vereins, 1876, p. 637.

9. See Kettler, op. cit., pp. 121 et seq.

10. Neumann, p. 495. Translation: 'Elegance precedes you, in order to strew your way with roses.'

11. My own doctoral dissertation (Cambridge, 1957) deals with the relationship of these words to others of a similar nature in German baroque literature.

12. See Forster's point about the Hoffmanswaldau poem quoted on p. 13 of his inaugural lecture, and in particular his remarks on the subject of Time, pp. 12–18.

13. Flemming, *Oper*, p. 33.

14. Flemming, *Orat. & Festsp.*, pp. 117–18.

CHAPTER IV.

1. Eulenburg Edition foreword, p. II.

2. See Manfred Bukofzer, 'Allegory in Baroque Music', *Journal of the Warburg Institute*, London, 1939–40, Vol. III, No. 1, pp. 1–21.

3. Arnold Schmitz, *Die Bildlichkeit der Wortgebundenen Musik Johann Sebastian Bachs*, Mainz: B. Schott's Söhne, 1949.

4. Walter Emery, 'Bach's Symbolic Language', *Music & Letters*, Vol. XXX, 1949, pp. 345 et seq.

5. Schmitz, p. 38.

6. See note 2, above.

7. Neumann, p. 18. Translation: 'Thy cheeks must shine much more beautifully today.'

8. See Hans Lenneberg, 'Johann Mattheson on Affect

and Rhetoric in Music', *The Journal of Music Theory*, Yale School of Music, Vol. II/1, April 1958, pp. 47 et seq.

9. Quoted in Schmitz, op. cit., footnote to p. 25.

10. Schmitz, op. cit., p. 26.

11. Flemming, *Orat. & Festsp.*, p. 20.

12. Lenneberg, p. 53.

13. See *The Pelican Guide to English Literature*, Vol. III, pp. 90–91.

SELECT BIBLIOGRAPHY

BENZ, R. *Die Kultur des 17. Jahrhunderts*, Stuttgart, 1949

BERGER, KURT. *Barock und Aufklärung im Geistlichen Lied*, Marburg, 1951.

BUKOFZER, M. 'Allegory in Baroque Music', *Journal of the Warburg Institute*, 1939–40, Vol. III/1.

———. *Music in the Baroque Era*, London, 1948.

CLERCX, SUSANNE. *Le Baroque et la Musique*, Brussels, 1948.

CLOSS, A. AND MAINLAND, W. F. (ed). *German Lyrics of the Seventeenth Century*, London, 1947.

DÜRR, A. 'Ueber Kantatenformen in den geistlichen Dichtungen Salomon Francks', *Musikforschung*, 1950, Vol. III, pp. 18 et seq.

EHRET, JOSEPH. *Das Jesuitendrama zu Freiburg in der Schweiz*, Freiburg i/B, 1921.

EMERY, WALTER. 'Bach's Symbolic Language', *Music & Letters*, 1949, Vol. XXX, pp. 345 et seq.

ERMATINGER, EMIL. *Deutsche Dichter, 1700-1900*, Frauenfeld, 1948.

FINLAY, IAN. 'Bach's Secular Cantata Texts', *Music & Letters*, 1950, Vol. XXXI, pp. 189 et seq.

FLEMMING, W. (ed.) Volumes 5 ('Die Oper') and 6 ('Oratorium und Festspiel') in *Deutsche Literatur in Entwicklungsreihen*, Reihe Barockdrama, Leipzig, 1933.

FORSTER, L. W. 'German Baroque Literature: A Synthetic View' (translation of an article by ERIK LUNDING), *German Life & Letters*, 1949, pp. 1–12.

———. *The Temper of Seventeenth Century German Literature*, London, 1952.

———— (ed.) *The Penguin Book of German Verse*, London, 1956.

HANNAM, T. *Notes on the Church Cantatas of J. S. Bach*, Oxford, 1928.

HEDERER, EDGAR. *Deutsche Dichtung des Barock*, Munich, 2nd. edition, 1957.

KETTLER, H. K. *Baroque Tradition in the Literature of the German Enlightenment, 1700–50*, Cambridge, 1946.

LANGEN, AUGUST. *Die Wortschatz des deutschen Pietismus*, Tübingen, 1954.

LENNEBERG, HANS. 'Johann Mattheson on Affect and Rhetoric in Music', *The Journal of Music Theory*, Vol. II/1, April 1958, Yale University.

DE MOURGES, ODETTE. 'The European Background to Baroque Sensibility', in Vol. III, *From Donne to Marvell*, of the *Pelican Guide to English Literature*, London, 1956, pp. 89 et seq.

MÜLLER, GÜNTHER. *Geschichte des deutschen Liedes vom Zeitalter des Barocks bis zur Gegenwart*, 1925.

NEUMANN, W. *Handbuch der Kantaten J. S. Bachs*, Leipzig, 1947.

————. *Johann Sebastian Bach Sämtliche Kantatentexte*, Leipzig, 1956.

NUGLISCH, O. *Barocke Stilelemente*, Berlin, 1938.

SCHERING, A. *Bach's Textbehandlung*, Leipzig, 1900.

————. *J. S. Bach's Leipziger Kirchenmusik*, Leipzig, 1936.

————. *Ueber Kantaten J. S. Bachs*, Leipzig, 1942.

SCHMITZ, A. *Die Bildlichkeit der wortgebundenen Musik J. S. Bachs*, Mainz, 1949.

SPERBER, HANS. *Die Sprache der Barockzeit*, Leipzig, 1929.

STRICH, FRITZ. *Der Barock*, Berne, 1946.

TAGLIAVINI, L. F. *Studie sui testi delle Cantate Sacre di J. S. Bach*, Milan/Padua; Cassel/Basel, 1956.

TERRY, C. S. *J. S. Bach's Cantata Texts, Sacred and Secular*, Oxford, 1926.

———. 'Bach's Cantata Libretti', *Proceedings of the Musical Assoc.*, Vol. XXIV, 1918.

———. *The Cantatas & Oratorios*, Musical Pilgrim, 2 Vols., Oxford, 1925.

TRUNZ, ERICH. 'Die Ueberwindung des Barock in der deutschen Lyrik', *Zeitschrift für Aesthetik*, 1941.

VIËTOR, KARL. *Problems der deutschen Barockliteratur*, Leipzig, 1928.

———. *Geschichte der deutschen Ode*, Leipzig, 1923.

WEHRLI, MAX. *Deutsche Barocklyrik*, Basel, 1945.

WHITTAKER, W. G. *Fugitive Notes on Certain Cantatas and the Motets of J. S. Bach*, Oxford, 1926.

WUSTMANN, R. *J. S. Bach's Kantatentexte*, Leipzig, 1914. Substantially the same as Neumann, but without the Secular Cantatas, and not nearly so easy to work with; layout is much less lucid.

INDEX